JANE AUSTEN

A BEGINNER'S GUIDE

JANE AUSTEN

A BEGINNER'S GUIDE

ROB ABBOTT
Series Editors
Rob Abbott and Charlie Bell

Hodder & Stoughton

A MEMBER OF THE HODDER HEADLINE GROUP

To David 'DJ' Bastable
An inspiring teacher

Orders: please contact Bookpoint Ltd, 130 Milton Park, Abingdon, Oxon OX14 4SB. Telephone:
(44) 01235 827720, Fax: (44) 01235 400454. Lines are open from 9.00–6.00, Monday to Saturday,
with a 24-hour message answering service. Email address: orders@bookpoint.co.uk

British Library Cataloguing in Publication Data
A catalogue record for this title is available from The British Library.

ISBN 0 340 80360 6

First published 2001
Impression number   10 9 8 7 6 5 4 3 2 1
Year   2007 2006 2005 2004 2003 2002 2001

Typeset by Transet Limited, Coventry, England.
Printed in Great Britain for Hodder & Stoughton Educational, a division of Hodder Headline
Plc, 338 Euston Road, London NW1 3BH by Cox & Wyman, Reading, Berks.

CONTENTS

Contents

How to use this book

The *Beginner's Guide* series aims to introduce readers to major writers of the past 500 years. It is assumed that readers will begin with little or no knowledge and will want to go on to explore the subject in other ways.

BEGIN READING THE AUTHOR

This book is a companion guide to Jane Austen's major works, it is not a substitute for reading the books themselves. It would be useful if you read some of the works in parallel, so that you can put theory into practice. This book is divided into sections. After considering how to approach the author's work and a brief biography, we go on to explore some of Austen's main writings and themes before examining some critical approaches to the author. The survey finishes with suggestions for further reading and possible areas of further study.

HOW TO APPROACH UNFAMILIAR OR DIFFICULT TEXTS

Coming across a new writer may seem daunting, but do not be put off. The trick is to persevere. Much good writing is multi-layered and complex. It is precisely this diversity and complexity which makes literature rewarding and exhilarating.

Literature often needs to be read more than once and in different ways. These ways can include: a leisurely and superficial reading to get the main ideas and narrative; a slower more detailed reading focusing on the nuances of the text, concentrating on what appear to be key passages; and reading in a random way, moving back and forth through the text to examine such things as themes, or narrative or characterization. Every reader has an individual approach but undoubtedly the best way to extract the most from a text is to read it several times.

With complex texts it may be necessary to read in short chunks. When it comes to tackling difficult words or concepts it is often enough to guess their meaning by context on the first reading, making a more detailed study using a dictionary or book of critical concepts on later readings. If you prefer to look up unusual words as you go along, be careful that you do not disrupt the flow of the text and your concentration.

VOCABULARY

You will see that keywords and unfamiliar words are set in **bold** text. These words are defined and explained in the glossary to be found at the back of the book. In order to help you further we have also included a summary at the end of each chapter.

You can read this introductory guide in its entirety or dip in wherever suits you. You can read it in any order. It is a tool to help you appreciate a key figure in literature. We hope you enjoy reading it and find it useful.

✳ ✳ ✳ SUMMARY ✳ ✳ ✳

To maximize the use of this book:

- Read the author's work.

- Read it several times in different ways.

- Be open to innovative or unusual forms of writing.

- Persevere.

Rob Abbott and Charlie Bell

Why read Jane Austen today?

STILL VERY RELEVANT

To read Jane Austen is to engage with history and yet also to see a world which we can clearly recognize as being like our own. It is a world which can seem ludicrously over-fussy, with its concerns about dress and manners, class and rank, etiquette and propriety. Yet its concern with morality, that is to say what is right and wrong, seems very modern, as does its focus upon relationships, love, trust, fidelity and betrayal which are as relevant today as they were in the nineteenth century. In reading Jane Austen we see the beginnings of our own age. The recent successes of film and television versions of her work and the continued popularity of her novels are testament to this modern relevance.

READ HER FOR HER HUMOUR

When we read a Jane Austen novel we enter a world that is lively, humorous, wonderfully entertaining and defined by a sophisticated ironical standpoint. Yet the ironical tone of so much of her work is also a source of contention and misunderstanding. Many readers don't realize at first that much of what is offered is meant to be deeply ironical and many critics argue over both the purpose and effect of this irony. It is undoubtedly a subtle tool. As we shall see later, some feminist critics make the point that irony is a characteristically feminine tool, a subversive weapon which is used to construct deliberately duplicitous readings. Yet there is a simpler level to irony too: if we understand it, then it can help us to laugh at human weaknesses and foibles.

READ HER FOR ENJOYMENT

One of the difficulties that new readers to Austen have is the problem of her 'greatness'. She is, along perhaps with George Eliot and Charles Dickens, one of the central pillars of the English novel. This elevation to the sublime can make it very hard simply to read her for enjoyment. Yet it is important to remember that she was certainly not regarded as great in her own lifetime, indeed it was not until her nephew's biography of her appeared in 1870 that her greatness was thrust upon her. There is also the terrible snobbishness associated with the ability to read and *enjoy* her. It is seen too often as a mark of intellectual prowess and aesthetic maturity to be able to gain pleasure from reading her novels.

The traditional view of Jane Austen is that of the secret scribbler, writing her novels in secret, hiding her words beneath the sofa whenever a door creaks. In effect, she is portrayed as a writer who deliberately cut herself off from the world around her. Whatever the truth of this, it is most certainly only one part of the picture. Austen was most consciously a writer who sought publication, who had a commercial interest and practical need to earn money from her writing and who was certainly very aware of the social, political and economic turns of the world in which she lived. The small income her family received after her father's death and her lack of an attractive dowry meant that her income from books was very important. She can be seen as a highly professional writer who produced novels at a time when conditions made it possible for female writers to succeed. These were writers such as Maria Edgeworth, Clara Reeve and Ann Radcliffe. That we read so few of these other female novelists today is another testament to Austen's worth.

The renewed interest in historical approaches to literature has enabled us to put Austen back into her context. We can see her as a writer who was very engaged with the political changes of her time. Studies such as *Jane Austen and the War of Ideas* by Marilyn Butler (1975) place Austen firmly in the centre of political debate. It is possible now to discuss this fascinating area of her work and to see her as a writer who was often very opposed to the massive social and political changes that were taking place at the turn of her century.

More so than most other writers, Austen has tended to be over-associated with her characters. One of the tasks of modern criticism is to tease apart this close link and think more critically. For example, does Austen like Elizabeth Bennet; approve of Emma; or have views about the implicit servitude in Emma's marriage to Mr Knightley? To ask and perhaps answer such questions is the purpose of this volume.

✻ ✻ ✻ SUMMARY ✻ ✻ ✻

- Austen's themes are still relevant today.

- Her novels are gloriously funny.

- Don't be put off by her 'greatness'.

- Explore her historical and political relevance.

2 How to approach Jane Austen

There are those who pick up their first Jane Austen and read with ever increasing joy and amusement and there are those who struggle through from a sense of duty or for a course of study and who never quite get the point. This chapter is an attempt to provide a few pointers on how to read an Austen novel.

IRONY

For a beginner, the most puzzling part of reading a Jane Austen novel is her use of **irony**. It is so hard to know when she is being serious and when she is gently (and often with great subtlety) mocking her characters, their thoughts, actions, words or even their feelings. Irony depends on the context of the writing and

> **KEYWORD**
>
> Irony: In simple terms, an expression of meaning in language which says one thing but suggests the opposite.

demands that we know enough about the characters and the story to spot that what is being said may be meant ironically. For this reason alone it is hard to pluck out bits of Austen's irony without describing in detail the context from which it comes. For example, we are told of Lady Bertram in *Mansfield Park*: 'To the education of her daughters, Lady Bertram paid not the smallest attention. She had not time for such cares.' This seems on the surface to be a straightforward description of a very busy, if somewhat uncaring, mother. It is only as we read more of the story that we realize that Lady Bertram in fact does absolutely nothing all day. She is a woman: '…who spent her days in sitting, nicely dressed, on a sofa, doing some long piece of needlework, of little use and no beauty' (both extracts from Chapter 2). What we have in this description of her is an example of Austen's savage and caustic irony.

So what is irony? It comes in many shapes and sizes but at a simple level irony exists where there are two or more meanings which can be implied from a piece of text. Often the underlying meaning will directly contradict the surface meaning. This is the case in the last example: Lady Bertram had plenty of time to care for her daughters *had she wished to do so*. It is her inherent idleness that is being mocked by Austen's irony here.

One of the most well-known examples of irony is contained in the opening to *Pride and Prejudice* which will be discussed in Chapter 5. Meanwhile, here is an extract from *Sense and Sensibility* in which Austen describes the first impressions created by the arrival of the Miss Steeles at Barton Park :

> The young ladies arrived: their appearance was by no means ungenteel or unfashionable. Their dress was very smart, their manners very civil, they were delighted with the house, and in raptures with the furniture, and they happened to be so doatingly fond of children that Lady Middleton's good opinion was engaged in their favour before they had been an hour at the Park. She declared them to be very agreeable girls indeed, which for her ladyship was enthusiastic admiration.
>
> (Volume 1, Chapter 21)

What are we to make of the Miss Steeles? Are we to take Austen at face value and think as highly of them as does Lady Middleton? They sound at first reading to be pleasant, clever, well-mannered girls. Yet Austen is in fact using a sharp ironic wit to highlight their shortcomings.

It is that first phrase 'their appearance was by no means ungenteel or unfashionable' that begins to give the game away. Why has Austen chosen to use a double negative here? Why not just say 'their appearance was genteel and fashionable'? Look at the way, too, that the language goes just that bit over the top: 'delighted' , 'in raptures', 'doatingly fond'. If we were in any doubt that this was all intended ironically then the observations of Elinor assure us that it was so:

'Elinor well knew that the sweetest girls in the world were to be met with in every part of England, under every possible variation of form, face, temper and understanding.'

FREE INDIRECT DISCOURSE

The single most important character in every Austen novel is the heroine. Whilst the novels are written in the third person, much of what the reader sees, hears and understands within the novel is mediated through the senses of the Austen heroine. This is achieved through the use of what is called **free indirect discourse**, whereby we are told without the reference point of direct quotation exactly what is being thought and felt by a character. Here, for example, is Emma's first meeting with her protégée, Harriet Smith:

> **KEYWORD**
>
> Free indirect discourse: A narrative style in which the narrator presents the thoughts of a character. The following is an example of direct speech, 'Emma said, "I am feeling unwell".' In indirect speech the sentence would be, 'Emma said she felt unwell.' In free indirect speech it would be simply, 'Emma felt unwell'.

Harriet Smith was the natural daughter of somebody. Somebody had placed her, several years back, at Mrs Goddard's school, and somebody had lately raised her from the condition of scholar to that of parlour-boarder. This was all that was generally known of her history. She had no visible friends but what had been acquired at Highbury, and was now just returned from a long visit in the country to some young ladies who had been at school there with her.

She was a very pretty girl, and her beauty happened to be of a sort which Emma particularly admired. She was short, plump, and fair, with a fine bloom, blue eyes, light hair, regular features, and a look of great sweetness, and, before the end of the evening, Emma was as much pleased with her manners as her person, and quite determined to continue the acquaintance.

She was not struck by any thing remarkably clever in Miss Smith's conversation, but she found her altogether very engaging – not inconveniently shy, not unwilling to talk – and yet so far from pushing, shewing so proper and becoming a deference, seeming so pleasantly grateful for being admitted to Hartfield, and so artlessly impressed by the appearance of every thing in so superior a style to what she had been used to, that she must have good sense, and deserve encouragement. Encouragement should be given. Those soft blue eyes, and all those natural graces, should not be wasted on the inferior society of Highbury and its connexions. The acquaintances she had already formed were unworthy of her. The friends from whom she had just parted, though very good sort of people, must be doing her harm.

(*Emma*, Volume 1, Chapter 3)

In the first paragraph we seem to be firmly in the hands of the narrator. We are told of Harriet's background and the perspective is that of the narrator with no direct evidence of Emma's viewpoint in the account of this history. In the second paragraph, however, we begin to move into the consciousness of Emma and see Harriet through her eyes. Her beauty is of the sort that Emma *admires*, Emma is 'much pleased' with Harriet's manners. Here the persona of the narrator seems to silently merge into that of Emma. It is as if the narrator stands behind Emma and begins to see the world through Emma's eyes.

The third paragraph is written totally in free indirect speech, we see Harriet exactly as Emma sees her and are privy to all her inner thoughts and resolutions concerning her new friend. The sentence 'Encouragement should be given' is Emma's assessment as is the notion that Harriet's current acquaintances are unworthy of her.

By taking us inside Emma's head, Austen is doing more than merely reporting her thoughts. Seeing what Emma is thinking allows Austen to explore one of the central concerns of this novel: the frailty of human judgement. What we perceive is too tainted by what we imagine or what we would like to see to allow us a stable version of events. And, of course, the process is more subtle still than a simple linear progression from an impartial narrator to an overly judgemental Emma. Look, for example, at the repetition of the word 'somebody' in the first paragraph of the extract. Is this purely a descriptive term for an unknown benefactor? Or does the repetition itself suggest a more judgemental stance?

SATIRE

As well as moments of the most subtle irony there are other moments when Austen is just plain funny. Nowhere is this more apparent than in her **satirizing** of the pompous and the stupid. Here, for example, is John Thorpe in *Northanger Abbey* extolling to Catherine Morland the virtues of his new carriage:

> **KEYWORD**
>
> Satire: To use satire is to ridicule often by exaggerating the traits of a character to expose them as failings or weaknesses. It is usually used for humorous effect but can often have a more serious purpose.

'What do you think of my gig, Miss Morland? A neat one, is not it? Well hung; town-built; I have not had it a month. It was built for a Christchurch man, a friend of mine, a very good sort of fellow; he ran it a few weeks, till, I believe, it was convenient to have done with it. I happened just then to be looking out for some light thing of the kind, though I had pretty well determined on a curricle too; but I chanced to meet him on Magdalen Bridge, as he was driving into Oxford, last term: "Ah! Thorpe," said he, "do you happen to want such a little thing as this? It is a capital one of the kind, but I am cursed tired of it." "Oh! D—," said I; "I am your man; what do you ask?" And how much do you think he did, Miss Morland?'

'I am sure I cannot guess at all.'

'Curricle-hung, you see; seat, trunk, sword-case, splashing-board, lamps, silver moulding, all you see complete; the iron-work as good as new, or better. He asked fifty guineas; I closed with him directly, threw down the money, and the carriage was mine.'

The humour here is less subtle than irony. Thorpe is an insensitive crushing bore whose only desire is to brag about the size, speed, and appearance of his curricle, oblivious to Catherine's complete lack of interest in the topic. He is the equivalent of today's motor car bore! Look at the technical language in the last paragraph of the extract and the tiresome attention to detail. Notice, too, that Thorpe answers his own question, without pausing for poor Miss Morland to say a word. And what a braggart too! He is full of himself and his possessions, never enquiring after her or paying her any attention at all other than as an audience for his audacity.

It is in her portrayal of the self-centred, the foolish and the ignorant that Austen achieves a perfection in her writing. Mr Collins, the boorish, arrogant and moronic vicar in *Pride and Prejudice* is a wonderful example of this as is his patroness, Lady Catherine de Bourgh. Look, for example, at the opening of Chapter 14 at the way Austen ridicules Collins's unctuous homage to Lady Catherine and the dry acerbity of Mr Bennet's answers. The arrogance of Sir Walter Elliot in *Persuasion* and of Mr and Mrs Elton in *Emma* or the hypocrisy of Mrs Norris in *Mansfield Park* are similarly ruthlessly satirized.

❋ ❋ ❋SUMMARY ❋ ❋ ❋

● Read Jane Austen for her humour and her style.

● Notice her effective use of irony to suggest the opposite of what she seems to say.

● Look out for her ruthless satirizing of the pompous and the stupid.

● Be aware of her use of free indirect discourse to take you into the thoughts of her characters.

---

3 Biography

AN ELUSIVE FIGURE

One of the difficulties faced by all biographers of Jane Austen is the scarcity of information about her and her life. She left no diary and little correspondence. There are some 160 letters written mostly to her sister, Cassandra and all written after the age of 20. It is believed that many others were destroyed by Cassandra after Jane's death in order to preserve her sister's privacy. The only other roughly contemporary source is the biography of Austen written some 50 years after she died by her nephew James Edward Austen-Leigh. It is a beautifully crafted biography, an excellent read, but Edward has sanitized the life of his aunt according to the sensibilities of Victorian England. Many other biographies have been trying since to re-examine the picture given to us by Austen-Leigh but she remains an elusive figure.

We have one description of her appearance. Austen-Leigh writes:

> In person she was very attractive; her figure was tall and rather slender, her step light and firm, and her whole appearance expressive of health and animation. In complexion she was a clear brunette with a rich colour; she had full round cheeks, with mouth and nose small and well formed, bright hazel eyes, and brown hair forming natural curls round her face.
>
> (Published as final section of *Persuasion*, Penguin Classics, p.330)

The one authentic watercolour sketch by Cassandra shows her with a bad-tempered, shrew-like expression, so unlike the picture we have of her from her writings, that a softened, revised version of it produced in the Victorian period is often displayed instead. The lack of real information about Jane Austen means that all biographies are highly speculative, often mixing fact and fantasy in about equal measure. Despite these problems and limitations it is still possible to present an account of her life, although it is harder to separate out the myth from the reality.

CHILDHOOD AND EDUCATION

Jane Austen was born in Steventon, Hampshire, on 16 December 1775. Her mother was Cassandra Leigh Austen and her father was George Austen, rector of Steventon. They belonged to the class known as 'lesser gentry', a rank some way below that of most of her fictional heroines. George Austen was also headmaster and sole teacher of a small boys' boarding school run from within the parsonage. At the age of seven Jane, along with her sister Cassandra, was plucked from her home environment and sent away to boarding school run by a Mrs Crawley, first in Oxford and then later in Southampton. By all accounts it was not a happy experience. In Southampton Jane fell ill and was eventually taken home and nursed back to health by her mother. After a year at home the girls were sent away to another school, the Abbey school in Reading. Towards the end of 1786 the girls were removed from the school and so, at about the age of 11, Jane finished her formal education.

The Austen home seems to have been a stimulating environment. Her father had a fairly good library and there was a tradition of performing family theatricals. These included a play called *Matilda*, a rather poor play by a Surrey clergyman and the much more stimulating *The Rivals* by Sheridan.

FIRST STEPS

Austen's first completed work is a now seldom read novel called *Lady Susan*. This is an **epistolary novel** and was written in the period 1793–4, when Jane was still in her teens. Soon after finishing this she began work on *Elinor and Marianne*, again written in letter form. Unfortunately, the manuscript of this early

KEYWORD

Epistolary novel: A novel written in the form of letters. Aphra Behn's *Love Letters between a Nobleman and his Sister* and Richardson's *Pamela* are two examples of the form.

forerunner of *Sense and Sensibility* has not survived but it is thought that it contained the idea of two sisters, one impetuous and the other more cerebral.

When Jane was 17, Cassandra became engaged to Tom Fowle, a clergyman who officiated at the wedding of a cousin. The story is a sad one. In 1795 Tom took a position as chaplain to a regiment that was posted to the West Indies. Two years later he was to die of yellow fever, leaving Cassandra distraught and Jane her main source of comfort.

In January 1796, Jane met a young man called Tom Lefroy from Ireland. It is believed that they were very attracted to each other and this is borne out in a letter to Cassandra where Jane refers to him as a 'gentlemanlike, good-looking, pleasant young man'. There is much speculation as to the feelings of both Jane and Tom, although it is known that they discussed Fielding's bawdy novel *Tom Jones* together. When he was an old man, Tom Lefroy told a nephew that he had felt a boyish love for the young Jane. Nothing was to come of the relationship, Lefroy returned to Ireland and the couple never met again.

It was soon after Tom's departure that Jane entered her first prolific period of writing. In October 1796, she began work on *First Impressions* and had finished it in nine months. In November 1797, she revised *Elinor and Marianne,* transforming it from the letter form into a standard third person narrative. This work was continued into 1798 and was eventually renamed *Sense and Sensibility.* In the following year she went to produce a first draft of what we now know as *Northanger Abbey.*

THE MOVE TO BATH

In 1800 the Austen family moved to Bath. It is believed that Jane was very unhappy at the prospect. Bath was at that time considerably less fashionable than its fictionalized counterpart in the novels. Certainly with a population of some 34,000 people it would have been a huge contrast to the quiet village of Steventon. The effect on Jane seems to have been profound, although this is another area of her life that is shrouded in some mystery. Letters written during the period in Bath show a peculiar sourness. It is thought that she may have suffered from depression during this period and for the first time in her life she stopped writing fiction. The death of her father five years later was another heavy blow which must have impacted on her fragile emotional state. Certainly his death left the family in dire financial circumstances. Mrs Austen and Cassandra had small incomes but Jane had none. Only one unfinished novel was written at this time, *The Watsons*.

OFFER OF MARRIAGE

In the December of 1802 Jane received and initially accepted a proposal of marriage from an old family friend Harris Bigg-Wither. Jane and Cassandra were close friends with Harris's sisters and what is more he was heir to a large estate. Jane would have no more financial worries and would also be able to offer a home to her sister. What seems to have been the flaw in this logic is that she felt no love for Harris Bigg-Wither. The next morning, after reportedly a sleepless night, she retracted her acceptance. Harris himself married two years later and eventually he and his wife produced ten children. Jane was to remain a spinster.

CHAWTON

The Austens returned to Hampshire in 1805 to a large rented house in Southampton. Then in 1808 they were offered a comfortable cottage in Chawton owned by Jane's brother, Edward. Here whatever muse that had been missing from Austen's life in Bath seemed suddenly to return. In the first year she revised both *Sense and Sensibility* and *Pride and Prejudice* and in the next five years had completed her three so-called 'mature' novels: *Mansfield Park*, *Emma* and *Persuasion*. She wrote mostly in the smaller sitting-room – the room with the now internationally famous door which squeaked whenever anyone entered. It thus played its part in keeping her writing career secret from all but a very few intimates. The closest of these intimates was undoubtedly her sister, Cassandra, although very little is known about her. Claire Tomalin describes her as 'a darkly seen shape' (*Jane Austen: A Life*, 1997, Viking, p. 195). She and Jane shared a room for the whole of their lives. She described Jane as 'the sun of my life, the girder of every pleasure' (quoted in *ibid*, p. 197). She was the only person with whom Jane discussed her work and most probably her only close confidante.

DEATH

In March 1817, after completing just 12 chapters, Jane Austen gave up her writing of the novel *Sanditon*. She had been ill for some time and it was decided that she should move to Winchester to be nearer her surgeon, Mr Lyford. The exact nature of her illness is unknown. Possibly it was Addison's disease, although other biographers have suggested breast cancer or lymphoma. She and Cassandra travelled the 16 miles from Chawton to Winchester in her brother James's carriage, accompanied by another brother, Henry, travelling on horseback. In Winchester her health steadily declined. She died in the early hours on 18 July, aged 41. She was buried in Winchester Cathedral near the centre of the north aisle, attended only by her family.

FAME

Jane Austen's fame came slowly. The publication of the Austen-Leigh biography in 1879 brought her to public notice and began the process of building her fame. It was the birth of what is now an Austen cult. Certainly since that period, her novels have remained continuously in print and her popularity has been constant.

* * * SUMMARY * * *

• Jane Austen was born in December 1775 and died in July 1817.

• She grew up in the tiny Hampshire village of Steventon where her father was the rector.

• The Austen family moved to Bath in 1800 where it is likely that Jane was very unhappy.

• She moved to Chawton in Hampshire in 1805.

The social scene

Jane Austen wrote her novels during the first two decades of the nineteenth century. George III had been on the throne since 1760. He was to reign until 1820, although for the last ten years of his life he was insane and so his son, later King George IV, was declared Prince Regent. Hence the period is known as the Regency period.

It was also a time that saw the end of the Agricultural Revolution and the beginning of the Industrial Revolution. It was a period of the great estates owned by wealthy families, fictionalized forms of which made up the backdrop to almost all Austen's novels: Pemberley (*Pride and Prejudice*); Mansfield Park, Norland Park and Barton Park (*Sense and Sensibility*), Donwell Abbey (*Emma*).

SOCIAL CLASS

Jane Austen's England was very class conscious. Indeed the whole social structure was still based on a class system that had been in existence in England for hundreds of years. It was beginning to change as the new middle classes, those who made their wealth in manufacturing and industry, began to seek (and at times demand) a higher social status, but in Austen's time theirs was a genteel voice. It was also a long time before political change began to enfranchize the ordinary man, let alone the ordinary woman.

At the top of the social pile were the royal family. Below them were the people known as 'the peerage' who were properly addressed as 'Lord' or 'Lady'. These were the dukes, marquesses, earls, viscounts and barons. Some way below these there were the knights and baronets whose formal address was 'Sir'. The vast majority of peerages at the time were hereditary. They were passed from father down to eldest son. Families

where there was no eldest son could pass the title sideways to another male member of the family. If there was no male descendent then the title would become extinct. Baronetcies were also hereditary whereas knighthoods (as is still the case) were only for life and could not be inherited. Members of the peerage had the right, along with the bishops and archbishops of the Church of England, to sit and vote in the House of Lords. Sir Walter Elliot in *Persuasion* is a baronet, a title which dates back to the first year of the reign of Charles II. Sir Thomas Bertram in *Mansfield Park* is another, although it is likely that his peerage is more recent, given his enthusiasm for marrying his daughters into more established families.

There were also what have been variously referred to as the 'middle-class aristocracy' or 'pseudo-gentry'. These were those who had made their money from trade and the professions but who aspired to the lifestyles of the traditional gentry. The Bingleys in *Pride and Prejudice* would fall into this class.

One means of raising your rank within the class system was by joining the Navy. Two of Austen's brothers, for example, rose to the rank of admiral and one received a knighthood in the process. The Navy also offered the possibility of considerable wealth in terms of prize money gained from captured vessels. Captain Wentworth in *Persuasion* returns considerably richer by 'successive captures' than he had been when he first proposed to Anne Elliot.

MONEY

It is not easy to get a sense of comparison between monetary values today and those in the late 1800s. For one thing labour was very cheap and so, comparatively at least, was property. It is therefore very difficult to compare like with like. On a Jane Austen website, *pemberley.com*, the pound in 1810 is compared to £27.28 today. This means that today, Darcy's £10,000 per year would be worth £272,800. Edward Copeland in a chapter entitled 'Money' in *The Cambridge Companion to Jane Austen* (edited by Copeland, E. and McMaster, J., 1997) provides a full account of the lifestyle which a range of incomes would have provided. At £500 a year a small family could afford to live comfortably with servants but no carriage. This luxury would become possible only at an income of above £700. With an income of £2,000 a year the Bennets (from *Pride and Prejudice*) could certainly afford a pleasant lifestyle, although this would not leave much with five daughters each needing a dowry! Above £4,000 a year, life becomes very comfortable indeed. This would have been the income of the Crawfords (*Mansfield Park*). Mr Darcy's great attraction was that he had an income of £10,000 a year. This was a huge amount of money and would place Darcy amongst the wealthiest 400 families in England. For the very wealthy such income came from land.

PRIMOGENITURE AND ENTAILING

Mr Bennet's problem in *Pride and Prejudice* is that when he dies his estate will not pass to his daughters, instead it is entailed to the obsequious Mr Collins. Entailing was a means of protecting the estate from being split up into smaller parcels of land. The great families who had so dominated English life for centuries could continue to do so only if their estates were not divided up when the wealth was passed from one generation to the next. The right of **primogeniture** meant that all the land in a family was left only to the eldest son. **Entailing** was a means of restricting what that son could do with it by insisting that when he died only his eldest son could inherit. An entailed estate could be neither sold nor mortgaged which meant that the heir could only continue to get income from the land. An estate could be entailed only across two generations so a grandfather could entail his estate to his grandson but not beyond. Thus the son could not sell any of it during his lifetime. The grandson, however, could do what he liked. In reality of course, a little gentle persuasion (or failing that a little coercion) usually forced the grandson into signing another deed entailing the estate to his own grandson. And so the great estates passed unchanged from one generation to the next.

KEYWORDS

Entailing restricted what a son could do with an estate when he inherited. It forced him to leave the land to his eldest son. An entailed estate could not be sold nor mortgaged and so could only be used for the purposes of maintaining an income by being farmed or rented. An estate could only be entailed across two generations so a grandfather could entail his estate to his grandson but not beyond.

The right of primogeniture meant that all the land in a family was left to only the eldest son.

SOCIETY BALLS

The ball in Jane Austen novels is the most favoured, most eagerly awaited social event that a young lady could hope for. It was of infinitely more significance than today's club, disco or rave. The ball in *Emma*, for example, is long anticipated, much prepared for and, as Austen reports, is dwelled on lovingly even before it is over:

> The ball proceeded pleasantly. The anxious cares, the incessant attentions of Mrs Weston, were not thrown away. Every body seemed happy; and the praise of being a delightful ball, which is seldom bestowed till after a ball has ceased to be, was repeatedly given in the very beginning of the existence of this.

(*Emma*, Volume 3, Chapter 2)

MARRIAGE

The importance of balls, of course, was the opportunity they afforded
to meet members of the opposite sex. A common criticism of Austen is
the emphasis she places in her novels on marriage and money. The aim
of every young woman, it would seem, is to marry and marry well. The
laws of primogeniture effectively excluded women from inheriting
property. The Bennet girls in *Pride and Prejudice* face the kind of stark
choice of many during the period: marry a wealthy man and live
comfortably or don't marry and live in penury. Marriage in reality was
not necessarily good news for a woman, despite the 'happily ever after'
endings of Austen's novels. Upon marriage all a woman's wealth went
to her husband. The only way she could retain wealth in her own right
was by remaining single.

TRAVEL

Travel during this period was much slower and more precarious than
it is today. This was a time before the railways when all journeys were
either on foot or by means of horse. Travel by horse and carriage was
slow. In *Persuasion*, for example, the 34-mile journey across country to
Lyme Regis and back during November is judged to take seven hours.
Even short distances by carriage could be difficult. The lack of street
lighting meant that evening social engagements such as dinner parties
were often held during periods of a full moon.

NAPOLEONIC WARS

Britain was at war with France on and off from 1793 until Napoleon
was finally defeated by Wellington at Waterloo in 1815. The periods of
war between 1800 and 1815 are known as the Napoleonic Wars as
France and her armies at this time were led by Napoleon Bonaparte.
There is some reference to these events in Austen's novels. For example,
soldiers in *Pride and Prejudice* are garrisoned near Longbourn as a
direct response to the threat of invasion by Napoleon's army. At that
time the south of England would have been flooded with militia as a
precaution against invasion. The militia were a body of men raised
specifically for the threat of invasion and was very different from the

regular army. This is seen when the errant Wickham finds respectability of a sort when he is transferred from the militia to the regulars (see *Pride and Prejudice*, Chapter 50).

GROWTH OF THE NOVEL

It is important to remember that the **novel** was still a very new and developing art form. Its popularity in the eighteenth century was partly at least associated with the growth of literacy amongst women. Certainly the romantic novel and the gothic novel (see Key fact page 23), were very popular with women readers. They were genres much favoured by women writers, which is perhaps why Austen chose to use both forms for her first fully realized novel, *Northanger Abbey*.

MANNERS AND ETIQUETTE

The codes of behaviour in Regency England were very different from those which we follow today. Part of the enjoyment of reading an Austen novel is in exploring the customs of a much more formal, more rigid society than that of Western Europe today.

> **KEYWORD**
>
> Novel: The modern novel developed quite slowly through the memoir novel and the epistolary novel (written in the form of letters) during the sixteenth and seventeenth century. Miguel de Cervantes *Don Quixote de la Mancha* (1605) is usually accepted as the first true novel. Daniel Defoe is regarded as the founder of the modern English novel, with *Robinson Crusoe* in 1719 and *Moll Flanders* in 1722.

Much of the scandal in Austen's novels is associated with those who get it wrong. Mr Collins in *Pride and Prejudice*, for example, speaks to Mr Darcy before he has been formally introduced, thus showing both Darcy and ourselves that he is no gentleman! Preparations for the play in *Mansfield Park* are considered an unsuitable activity in general, but particularly so for Maria. As an engaged lady she should not be acting so frivolously, particularly as certain scenes involve her touching a man who is not her fiancé! The disastrous matchmaking by the eponymous Emma is viewed, in part, with great horror by Mr Knightley because Harriet Smith is of the wrong social class to be matched with either Mr Elton or Mr Churchill.

As to the behaviour of Austen's scoundrels, for example, Willoughby (*Sense and Sensibility*) and Wickham (*Pride and Prejudice*), the scurrilous nature of it shocked and offended readers in the nineteenth century much as it does now. Willoughby, particularly in his seduction and abandonment of the 16-year-old ward of Colonel Brandon, both deserves and gets our condemnation as soundly as he gets that of Elinor. As for the heartless William Elliot in *Persuasion*, he is presented without mercy:

> Mr Elliot is a man without heart or conscience; a designing, wary, cold-blooded being, who thinks only of himself; whom for his own interest or ease, would be guilty of any cruelty, or any treachery, that could be perpetrated without risk of his general character.

> (*Persuasion*, Chapter 21)

In these words, spoken by Mrs Smith whom Elliot has defrauded, there is no irony, no satire, just plain and pithy condemnation. Elliot is condemned as is Willoughby and Wickham. There is in the Austen novel a reassuring sense of right and wrong, although as you might expect, modern criticism has questioned whether everything is always quite as straightforward as it seems! (See Chapter 8 for an exploration of modern approaches to Austen.)

✳ ✳ ✳ SUMMARY ✳ ✳ ✳

- Jane Austen's England was very class conscious.

- Entailing meant that the rich were able to pass their wealth from one generation to the next.

- Travel was undertaken by horse or on foot and was very slow.

- Aspects of the wars with France can be found in Austen's novels.

- The novel was a new and developing form.

- Manners were more formal and codes of behaviour stricter than they are today.

5 Major works – early novels

All of Jane Austen's novels are concerned with the struggle of a heroine (or, in the case of *Sense and Sensibility,* heroines) to find a suitable husband. Each novel begins with a woman in a position of some vulnerability implicitly or explicitly in search of a husband. A series of problems, often associated with initially choosing the wrong man, are overcome and the novels conclude with the sound of wedding bells and a sense of living happily ever after. This is a very traditional form of love story – poor and/or misguided girl is at first repelled and then charmed by rich(er), older man. The most archetypal of these is, of course, *Pride and Prejudice.* The novels provide six variations on this theme ranging from the instant attractions portrayed in *Northanger Abbey* to the much slower and problematic journeys towards resolution seen in the later novels. Whilst Tilney and Catherine (*Northanger Abbey*) are attracted from the start it is much more problematic to trace the course of the romance between Emma and Mr Knightley (*Emma*). One characteristic of the genre is that the path of true love is always narrow, crooked and uneven!

NORTHANGER ABBEY

Northanger Abbey is usually seen as the earliest of Jane Austen's novels, although it was not published until after her death. It is certainly her most youthful novel, partly because its heroine, Catherine Morland, is aged only 17 and partly because stylistically and structurally there are signs of immaturity. For example, the obscure reference to the name Richard in the opening paragraph is a rather awkwardly placed family joke. The unsatisfactory development of Catherine as a character is another example of this immaturity. Certainly there is in the novel a lightness of tone, one consequence of which has been that it has attracted far less serious critical attention than any of the other five completed novels.

A major problem with the novel is that it contains two stories that seem to be welded together abruptly in the middle. Perhaps this was so. You will need to decide for yourself. Was Jane Austen deliberately using the two contrasting settings and main stories to show the shallowness of the social world, and of how a giddy and innocent young girl can easily be misled by her fancies? Or is this an early piece of writing adapted and added to in later life by a more mature writer? You might wish to search the novel for clues.

KEYWORD

Burlesque: The ridiculing of an existing form of writing, traditionally by treating a serious subject in a light-hearted way. In writing a burlesque of the gothic form Austen is mocking the far-fetched plots and clichéd scenarios that many of these novels adopt.

The first part of the story recounts Catherine's stay in the fashionable Bath of the 1790s. Catherine is the daughter of a respectable clergyman and is taken to Bath by Mr and Mrs Allen, partly, if not wholly, for the purposes of romance. She quickly meets the eligible young clergyman Henry Tilney, son of the tyrannical General Tilney. She is attracted to Henry and also establishes a friendship with his sister, Eleanor. Here she also meets John Thorpe, a friend of her brother's and his sister, Isabella. Her friendship with the vain and manipulative Isabella and its eventual end forms a crucial part of the growing up which Catherine undergoes in the novel. The second part of the story concerns Catherine's visit to the Tilney's home, Northanger Abbey. Here there is both the resolution of the love story between Catherine and Henry and also a **burlesque** of the **gothic novel** so popular at the end of the eighteenth century.

KEY FACT

Gothic novel: The first true gothic novel was Horace Walpole's *The Castle of Otranto*, published in 1765. It was a form that became very popular in the second half of the eighteenth century. The stories usually involve a frail, beautiful heroine who finds herself stranded and alone in a haunted castle, abbey, graveyard or other unlikely place. Given these circumstances such heroines tend to scream and/or faint and usually invite rescue, preferably from the dashing young hero. Ann Radcliffe's novel *The Mysteries of Udolpho*, with its wild and highly improbable plot, was a particular success in the 1790s and is the novel most consciously parodied in *Northanger Abbey*. The form has been developed by both nineteenth- and twentieth-century writers. Charlotte Brontë's *Villette* and Mary Shelley's *Frankenstein*, for example, use and develop the genre and it has influenced the modern day English magical realist writers such as Emma Tennant and Angela Carter.

Starting the book

The opening of *Northanger Abbey* establishes
Catherine Morland as a very ordinary young
woman and, as such, one who is at considerable
variance to the typical heroine of the gothic
romance. Indeed Austen goes to considerable
lengths to distinguish her heroine from any that
might be expected by the very gothic title of the
novel. Her father, we are told was 'not in the
least addicted to locking up his daughters', a
much favoured activity in the gothic world; her

mother, again contrary to the gothic tradition, has survived Catherine's
birth. These traditions are affirmed later in the gothic section of the
novel. Here, Eleanor Tilney's imposed obedience to her father's wishes
amounts to a virtual imprisonment. This, and the loss of her mother
when Eleanor was 13, is the subject of much fearful speculation by the
impressionable young Catherine.

Catherine's ordinariness in her childhood, her aversion to becoming
'accomplished' is much dwelt upon in the opening paragraphs of the
novel. Austen seems determined to establish Catherine's inability to be
anything other than very plain. She cannot learn music, is unable to
draw, cannot memorize poetry without considerable effort and is
unremarkable in either writing or arithmetic. Even her appearance is
plain for she, 'had a thin awkward figure, a sallow skin without colour,
dark lank hair, and strong features' (Chapter 1). Yet at 15 she begins to
change and from 15 to 17 she begins her training for a heroine. The
account of Catherine's development is rich in self-mocking parody.
Whatever qualities of heroism are eventually to be bestowed upon
Catherine it is clear that they will have close associations with
literature. What is interesting about the choice of quotations supplied
by Austen is not just that so many of them are misquotes (usually seen
as inadvertent rather than purposeful) but that they are so deliberately

useless. As a range of **aphorisms** designed to be both 'serviceable' and 'soothing' they would seem to fall well short of either target! The choice here establishes that Catherine's performance as a heroine will owe more to the realm of literature than to reality and that as such it is likely to be woefully inadequate.

> **KEYWORD**
>
> Aphorism: A pithy expression, saying or maxim.

The Bath scenes

The first part of the book (Chapters 2–19) is set in Bath and is as much a comedy of manners as a love story. Look, for example, at the scene where Catherine first meets Henry Tilney in Chapter 3. Here there is the same self-conscious parody as we saw in the opening chapter. Tilney apologizes to Catherine for being 'very remiss … in the proper attentions' and proceeds to list the precise questions a young man should pose to a young lady upon their first acquaintance. Having listed these he then delivers them in a mock-serious style. One of the delights, and one of the difficulties, in reading *Northanger Abbey* is in determining the degree to which it requires us to take it seriously. The novel seems continually to be setting itself up as a parody. As a consequence, we as readers are both engaging with it as a story but also sitting with the author just outside the narrative commenting upon it as an artifice. This seems particularly true with scenes involving Henry Tilney.

A book about books

The self-consciousness of the fiction is furthered by the continual references to literature in general and fiction in particular within the novel. The book, more than any other Austen novel, is a book about books. The diatribe about novels in Chapter 5 and the discussion about reading at Beechen Cliff (Chapter 14) are two examples of this. As Marilyn Butler shows in her introduction to the Penguin Classic edition of the novel, Austen has assumed a certain amount of literary knowledge in her readers if they are to appreciate the range and depth of parody within the narrative.

The gothic scenes

For many chapters in Ann Radcliffe's *The Mysteries of Udolpho* we follow the heroine, Emily, as she is pursued or led around the castle in fearful expectation of either her life or her modesty. Yet, despite all the expectation that

KEYWORD

Bathos: A descent from the elevated to the commonplace for comic effect.

such a journey arouses, nothing actually happens to her at all. In *Northanger Abbey* the same **bathos** is used to considerable comic effect. Austen employs many references to this novel and others by Ann Radcliffe to first establish in both Catherine's and the reader's mind all the dark and sinister elements of the gothic novel. Henry's vivid yet playful picture of a young lady's stay in a gothic home (Chapter 20) is sufficient to stir Catherine's imagination. The language he employs in describing this imagined horror is that of the genre itself. 'After surmounting your *unconquerable* horror of the bed, you will retire to rest', he tells the terrified Catherine. Peals of thunder will 'shake the edifice to its foundation'. She will discover hidden doors to vaulted rooms containing daggers, blood and instruments of torture.

The story he tells of the imagined dangers of such a stay and the language he adopts prefigure and promote the language used by Austen in the succeeding chapter where Catherine explores for herself the terrifying horrors of her bed-chamber. Here Catherine finds the objects which Tilney has pre-empted. There is a 'large high chest' (all quotations from Chapter 21) partially hidden from view. To make matters worse the night is stormy causing the curtains to move, the wind to roar down the chimney and the rain to beat against the window. It is the 'high, old-fashioned black cabinet', so like the ebony cabinet previously described by Henry, that becomes the centre of Catherine's over-stretched imagination. As she attempts to force open the locks of the cabinet we are told, 'Catherine's heart beat quick, but her courage did not fail her.' As she finds a piece of paper, a 'precious manuscript' hidden 'apparently for concealment' her excitement and terror rises until:

Her heart fluttered, her knees trembled, and her cheeks grew pale. She seized, with an unsteady hand, the precious manuscript, for half a glance sufficed to ascertain written characters; and while she acknowledged with awful sensations this striking exemplification of what Henry had foretold, resolved instantly to peruse every line before she attempted to rest.

As the episode reaches its climax Austen allows her heroine to impose her own dramatic cliff-hanger. In trying to remove the burnt part of the wick she extinguishes the candle and is thus left in traditional gothic terror hearing hollow murmurs, 'her blood ... chilled by the sound of distant moans.' Only in the cooling light of morning does she discover that all she has found is a laundry list!

PRIDE AND PREJUDICE

Pride and Prejudice is the most popular and certainly the most easily enjoyed of Austen novels. It was originally written in the 1790s as a book called *First Impressions* and sent to Cadell publishers in London in 1797. The novel was rejected and was rewritten some ten years later as *Pride and Prejudice* and published in a first edition of about 1,500 copies in January 1813. It sold out, as did a second and a third edition. Whilst it was not a big seller (by comparison, say, with Walter Scott's novels which were published and sold out in batches of 10,000) it did well for a first novel and Austen was from the start 'well regarded'.

The new title almost certainly comes from the ending of Fanny Burney's *Cecilia:*

Yet this, however, remember: if to PRIDE AND PREJUDICE you owe your miseries, so wonderfully is good and evil balanced, that to PRIDE AND PREJUDICE you will also owe their termination. [Original capitalization]

(*Cecilia*, Book 10, Chapter 10)

The story is at surface level a simple one and one much favoured by eighteenth-century novelists. It is the tale of a girl who is poor, relatively at least, who meets and eventually marries a man who is both wealthy and considerably above her in terms of social position. Whilst they are initially antagonistic towards each other these feelings soon change. First we witness Darcy's unwilling fascination for Elizabeth and her vehement rejection of his proposal. Then, later, we see Elizabeth's feelings perform a complete turn about until we arrive at what some would see (although not all) as the classic happy ever after ending. Yet if this was all there was to the story, it is likely that it would have sunk into the same oblivion as all those other eighteenth- and nineteenth-century love stories.

The famous opening
Pride and Prejudice has one of the most famous opening sentences in English literature:

> It is a truth universally acknowledged, that a single man in possession of a good fortune must be in want of a wife.

What are we to make of this as the beginning of a novel? It has first of all that wonderful Austen irony – it doesn't mean quite what it seems to mean. We can begin to unpick the irony (and thus the humour) by questioning the text. Is this a truth? In what sense is it 'universally acknowledged'? Is it only rich single men who seek wives? What about poor men? It quickly becomes obvious that this is neither a truth nor a universally held viewpoint. This becomes further apparent as Austen warms to her theme:

> However little known the feelings or views of such a man may be on his first entering a neighbourhood, this truth is so well fixed in the minds of the surrounding families, that he is considered the rightful property of someone or other of their daughters.

And here we find the origin of this truth and the extent of its universality. The man it seems has little say in the matter one way or another; it is a truth only in the minds of surrounding families, particularly those who find themselves in need of husbands for their one or more daughters!

The opening, too, has something of the formality of a prologue. The theatrical roots of this term are further emphasized by the theatrical form of the rest of the first chapter. Apart from the opening and closing paragraphs it is almost all dialogue. Although stylistically the novel does not continue with this form, the opening chapter provides a theatrical as well as a dramatic start to the narrative. The effect of the theatrical form here is to opening the novel with a suddenness, as if we had just walked into the Bennet's drawing room to find them in the middle of a conversation.

The arrogance of Darcy

We meet Darcy in the third chapter of the novel. Austen establishes him immediately as a highly eligible bachelor both in terms of looks and income:

> Mr Darcy soon drew the attention of the room by his fine, tall person, handsome features, noble mien, and the report which was in general circulation within five minutes after his entrance, of his having ten thousand a year.

Such eligibility only lasted, we are told, for the first half of the evening at which point 'his manners gave a disgust' and he is found to be proud. For the reader, too, the rise and fall of Darcy is a rapid one, accomplished indeed in one short paragraph and condemned for us in the next by the Meryton assembly who quickly conclude that he is the 'most disagreeable man in the world'. Further confirmation for the reader soon follows. As you read this chapter, note that this is the reader's first foray into the thoughts of Elizabeth Bennet. It is written not in free indirect speech but as direct speech, a conversation overheard word for word. We hear exactly what Elizabeth hears as Darcy contemptuously dismisses the women at the ball and says of Elizabeth, 'She is tolerable, but not handsome enough to tempt *me*' (Chapter 3). That we witness this from Elizabeth's viewpoint is established by the paragraph that precedes the conversation in which we see Elizabeth sitting 'near enough to overhear' and by the fact that her reaction to it is described immediately afterwards.

Away from the earshot of Elizabeth Bennet, Darcy is further shown to the reader to be as he appears to Meryton:

> Darcy was clever. He was at the same time haughty, reserved, and fastidious, and his manners, though well-bred, were not inviting. In that respect his friend had greatly the advantage. Bingley was sure of being liked wherever he appeared, Darcy was continually giving offence.

It is thus established early in the novel that Darcy, although rich and handsome, is disliked by Meryton society in general and by Elizabeth in particular.

A story of revelation

Yet *Pride and Prejudice* is a story of change. It is not until both central **protagonists** are able to change from their initial positions of prejudicial certainty and accept their own fallibility that they will each ensure happiness.

> **KEYWORD**
>
> Protagonist: The chief character in a play or story.

For Darcy the change begins early. It is also soon established that, dislikeable though he may be, Darcy's original condemnation of Elizabeth as 'not handsome enough' is, not to last. He is beguiled initially by the 'beautiful expression of her dark eyes' (Chapter 6) and later by her wit and cleverness. For Elizabeth there are no redeeming features either in Darcy's physical features or in his manners.

As in all of Austen's novels our view of events is seen primarily through the eyes of the heroine. Thus, we too see the world through Elizabeth's eyes. We learn to value her wit and intelligence. We also find, as she does, Darcy's arrogance all too much to bear. Whilst for both the reader and Elizabeth there is not quite a single moment of revelation, it is the scene in which Darcy so arrogantly proposes to Elizabeth that can be taken as the starting point of the transformation.

Darcy's proposal is conceited and insulting:

> 'In vain I have struggled. It will not do. My feelings will not be repressed. You must allow me to tell you how ardently I admire and love you.'
>
> (*Pride and Prejudice*, Chapter 34)

It is rejected summarily and angrily by Elizabeth, who tells him not only why she rejects his proposal but also why she despises his attitudes and his behaviour towards both her sister and the beguiling Mr Wickham. Darcy is astonished that his proposal of marriage to Elizabeth should be so savagely rejected. His pride is actively humbled by her rejection. Much later when the lovers are reconciled he admits:

'The recollection of what I then said, of my conduct, my manners, my expressions during the whole of it, is now, and has been for many months, inexpressibly painful to me. Your reproof, so well applied, I shall never forget…'

(Pride and Prejudice, Chapter 58)

Just as Elizabeth teaches Darcy the lesson of humility so, too, he returns the lesson. In his letter he shows her just how misguided her own appraisal of events has been. 'Till this moment I never knew myself', she cries acknowledging the revelatory nature of this experience (Chapter 36).

In his analysis of Austen's work, Tony Tanner points to this moment as the start of Elizabeth's education but suggests that it doesn't come to an end until she has penetrated Pemberley and seen the Darcy portrait:

> Standing before the large and true image of the real Darcy, Elizabeth has in effect completed her journey. When she next meets the original, outside in the grounds, she is no longer in any doubt as to his true worth.
>
> (Tanner, T., Jane Austen, 1986, Macmillan, p. 120)

The original title of the book, First Impressions, still captures the essence of the story. It is a tale of how first impressions can so often be wrong. However, this is not always the case and the first impressions created by the likes of Mr Collins and Lady Catherine de Bourgh are confirmed as correct. But for both Darcy and Elizabeth their views of each other must turn through a complete 180 degrees before the novel can reach its ultimate happy conclusion.

SENSE AND SENSIBILITY

Sense and Sensibility begins in familiar Austen territory – the problem of inheritance and wealth. The threat that hangs over the Bennet girls in Pride and Prejudice, that of losing their father and thus their family home and most of their wealth, becomes a reality in Sense and Sensibility.

The story begins with a series of deaths. First old Mr Dashwood dies a bachelor, leaving a life interest in the estate to his nephew, Mr Henry Dashwood, with the long-term ownership entailed to Henry's son and grandson. The death a year later of Henry Dashwood means the estate passes to his son John (whose son in turn will later inherit). This leaves the second Mrs Henry Dashwood and her two daughters, Elinor and Marianne, both without a home and in some financial difficulty.

Of the new owner of Norland, John Dashwood, we are told:

> He was not an ill-disposed young man, unless to be rather cold-hearted and rather selfish is to be ill-disposed: but he was, in general, well-respected; for he conducted himself with propriety in the discharge of his ordinary duties.
>
> (*Sense and Sensibility*, Chapter 1)

In Austen's heavily ironic account we follow the thoughts of John Dashwood and his wife ('a strong caricature of himself; – more narrow-minded and selfish') as they persuade themselves that the widow and her daughters can manage perfectly adequately on the £500 a year with which they are now left and that additional help from himself would 'be absolutely unnecessary, if not highly indecorous' (Chapter 2). Having lost the Norland estate (note the name – they have neither wealth *nor land*) Mrs Dashwood and her two daughters are offered a small house in the grounds of Barton Park, a small estate owned by a relative, Mr Middleton.

At Barton Park, Marianne meets the dashing Willoughby and falls very desperately in love. When he disappears to London she is heart-broken, a state worsened by his lack of communication. When Elinor and Marianne eventually go to London to stay with the tactless Mrs Jennings, they hope to renew his acquaintance. However, he brutally announces to Marianne in a letter 'which proclaimed its writer to be deep in hardened villainy' (Volume 2, Chapter 2) his engagement to a rich heiress. Elinor subsequently discovers that Edward Ferrars, the man she was almost engaged to, is also betrothed to the rather vacuous Lucy. The untangling of these events, the exposure of Willoughby as a truly unprincipled rogue, the nobleness and generosity of Colonel Brandon and the eventual happy ending are the business of the second part of the novel.

The binary opposition of Marianne and Elinor

There would seem to be a clear binary opposition in *Sense and Sensibility* between the two sisters, Elinor and Marianne, the one with too much sense and the other with too much sensibility. One way to understand the novel is to look at the differences and similarities of these two sisters. For Robert Clark the split is both defining and deterministic:

> In *Sense and Sensibility*, Austen splits her inclinations into a rationalist who is always right, and a passionate, emotional woman who can only be wrong, and the antithetical opposition of these two inclinations predetermines a conclusion in which the rationalist will repress the romantic.
>
> (Clark, R., *New Casebook: Sense and Sensibility and Pride and Prejudice*, 1994, Macmillan, p. 9)

Some critics suggest that the two are much more similar than this, whilst Ros Ballaster, in her introduction to the Penguin Classics edition, suggests that the split is not between opposites but rather that Elinor is Marianne's 'better half' (p. xiii).

The central difference between the two sisters would seem to be presented as one of control rather than inclination. The differences between these two sisters are made apparent throughout the novel not least because, as many have commented, they both go through the same range of experiences. Both believe themselves to be as good as, if not actually, engaged to men and both find themselves spurned by these men in favour of another. This similarity of experience serves only to emphasize the differences between their two characters. Indeed Austen goes to considerable lengths to accentuate their differences. The concluding paragraphs of Chapter 1 stress Elinor's sense of control: 'her feelings were strong: *but she knew how to govern them*' [added emphasis]. Marianne is shown to be similar in many ways but has one important difference: 'Her sorrows, her joys, could have no moderation.' This difference between the two women is most clearly drawn in the way each is shown to deal with the discovery of their lover's duplicity.

When Elinor hears from Lucy, in Chapter 22, that she is engaged to Edward she merely turns towards her, 'in silent amazement'. Her only physical coloration is contained by the phrase 'her complexion varied'. Her control is remarkable. We are told, 'she stood firm in incredulity and felt no danger of an hysterical fit, or a swoon.' Austen emphasizes that it is self-control which distinguishes Elinor's reaction. Her heroine speaks 'cautiously' and 'with a calmness of manner, which tolerably well concealed her surprise and solicitude'. Austen tells us that Elinor was 'mortified, shocked, confounded' yet it is not until she is alone that she is 'at liberty to think and be wretched'. Yet we as readers see none of this wretchedness. This phrase ends the first volume of the novel and when we see Elinor again it is as she is engaged not in wretchedness but rather upon 'serious reflection'. Whatever self-control we may wish to imagine as being lost is contained safely within that gap in the narrative. In considerable contrast, we witness every moment of Marianne's distress.

Marianne's reaction is shown to be everything that Elinor's is not. For Marianne there is no control. Her face, we are told, 'crimsoned over' and she speaks 'in a voice of the greatest emotion'. She cries out 'in the wildest anxiety'. Unlike the account of her sister's crisis we are taken behind the scenes to witness the private grief – for her distress is shared both by her sister and by the reader. The extremity of Marianne's reaction is emphasized in a number of ways. There is firstly the cold rejection of Willoughby's letter immediately followed by Elinor's indignant condemnation of the writer. There is secondly Marianne's hysteria: '…covering her face with her handkerchief, [she] almost screamed with agony.' And then lastly we are presented with Marianne's three letters to Willoughby proceeding from the playful vulnerability of the first through to the accusatory remorse of the last.

Even so, having been spurned, both sisters seek to excuse their lovers' behaviour. Marianne's, 'I could rather believe every creature of my acquaintance leagued together to ruin me in his opinion, than believe his nature capable of such cruelty' is expressed in a more emotive spirit than Elinor's '…Edward had done nothing to forfeit her esteem…' but the sentiments remain the same.

Marriage

Like all Austen novels, *Sense and Sensibility* ends in the marriage of the heroine. Yet marriage in this novel does not seem a necessarily desirable state. As Rachel M. Brownstein points out, the presentations of more established marriages in the novel are fairly dark. There is the selfishness of John and Fanny Dashwood as well as the unsuitability of the Middletons and Palmers, whose relationship causes Elinor to reflect upon 'the strange unsuitableness which often existed between husband and wife' (*Sense and Sensibility*, Chapter 21). The 'happy ending' would also seem to be neither quite as happy nor as straightforward as we might expect. As is Austen's custom, the marriages themselves at the end of the novel take place outside the narrative. Of Elinor's wedding we are told only that 'the ceremony took place in Barton Church early in the autumn' (Volume 3, Chapter 14). Marianne's marriage is not related, we are merely told: 'she found herself at nineteen, submitting to new attachments, entering on new duties, placed in a new home, a wife, the mistress of a family, and the patroness of a village' (Volume 3, Chapter 14). Even Edward's long-awaited proposal is deliberately excluded from the narrative:

How soon he had walked himself into the proper resolution, however, how soon an opportunity of exercising it occurred, in what manner he

expressed himself, and how he was received, *need not be particularly told.*
[Emphasis added]

(Volume 3, Chapter 13)

We are asked to believe that the marriages of Elinor and Marianne are happy ones. Even this, as Brownstein points out is far from unambiguous:

> ... the concluding paragraph brilliantly undoes the requisite romantic resolution, by startlingly giving Elinor's and Marianne's attachment to one another pride of place, so to make their second attachments, to their husbands, seem merely secondary.

(In Copeland, E. and MacMaster, J. (eds)
The Cambridge Companion to Jane Austen, 1997, CUP p. 48)

Certainly the marriage of Marianne to a man 20 years her senior and to whom she has exchanged hardly a word throughout the course of the novel leaves the reader with a sense that such a marriage is a tidy ending but not necessarily a convincing one.

✳ ✳ ✳ SUMMARY ✳ ✳ ✳

- All of the books are concerned with the struggle of a heroine to find a husband.

- *Northanger Abbey* is a parody of two very different styles – the romantic love story and the gothic horror.

- *Pride and Prejudice* is a story of revelation. Both central characters undergo their own process of revelation before the story can be resolved.

- *Sense and Sensibility* is a story of oppositions. The relationship of the two sisters is central to the development of the novel.

6 Major works – later novels

TWO TYPES OF HEROINE

In *Jane Austen and The War of Ideas* Marilyn Butler suggests there are two plots in the Austen novels based upon the two distinct types of heroine. There is the plot involving the heroine who is right – Elinor, Fanny and Anne. These heroines are seen by Butler as advocating self-sacrifice and the principle of duty. They are also seen as speaking for Christian orthodoxy. The other plot involves the heroines who are wrong – Catherine, Elizabeth and Emma. In these novels it is only after the heroine has discovered that she is wrong that the plot can be resolved. In both Emma and Elizabeth's case, it is pride and presumption which have to be encountered and overcome; with Catherine it is simply immaturity and her confusion of fiction with the real world which need to be conquered:

> The difference between the two types of plot does not lie in the action but the relationship of the central character to the action. In the one case the heroine makes a moral discovery, in the other she brings it about in someone else.
>
> (1975, Clarendon Press, p. 166)

Of the three so-called 'mature' novels, it is *Mansfield Park* which maintains the most consistently conscious moral tone. Fanny may be a heroine who is right but she is also the Austen heroine most likely to exasperate.

MANSFIELD PARK

Mansfield Park is generally regarded as Jane Austen's most difficult and complex work. It is certainly the novel that is hardest to enjoy at first reading, if also the one that benefits most from rereading. It was written in 1813 although it is set in the 1770s. Its heroine, Fanny Price, is the least popular of all Austen's heroines. She is often seen as too priggish, too delicate and far too inactive and timid to be any sort of heroine at all.

Appearance and reality

One way of reading the novel is to see it as an exploration of the differences and tensions between surface appearance and an underlying reality. It does this in several ways – most directly by pointing to the dichotomy that often exists between action and thought. These differences are also shown by Austen's familiar use of irony in describing characters other than Fanny. For example, here is the narrative voice commenting on the meanness of Mrs Norris:

> As far as walking, talking, and contriving reached, she was thoroughly benevolent, and nobody knew better how to dictate liberality to others; but her love of money was equal to her love of directing, and she knew quite as well how to save her own as to spend that of her friends.
>
> (*Mansfield Park*, Chapter 1)

The attack here is unambiguous and cutting. It points to the hypocrisy of Mrs Norris, seen in her tendency freely to offer advice but rarely offer action. It also directs our attention to her meanness, a quality that becomes her motif as the novel develops.

In *Mansfield Park* (more than in any other novel) a second device is used – that of **symbolism**. Its use is most apparent in the scenes showing rehearsals for the play *Lovers' Vows* but is also apparent in many other less significant scenes. For example, here is Fanny talking to Mary Crawford:

KEYWORD

Symbolism: The use of an image or concept to represent another. In its simplest sense this is where one object is used to represent another, for example, a thunderstorm to represent extremes of emotion. Often, though, the relationship between the symbol and what it represents is a complex one.

'This is pretty, very pretty,' said Fanny, looking around her as they were thus sitting together one day; 'every time I come into this shrubbery I am more struck with its growth and beauty. Three years ago, this was nothing but a rough hedgerow along the upper side of the field, never thought of as anything, or capable of becoming anything; and now it is converted into a walk, and it would be difficult to say whether most valuable as a convenience or an ornament and perhaps, in another three years, we may be forgetting – almost forgetting what it was before.'

(*Mansfield Park*, Chapter 22)

In speaking of the miraculous changes that have happened to the shrubbery Fanny is commenting, apparently without consciousness, on the changes that have also happened to her. When she arrived at Mansfield Park she was 'never thought of as anything, or capable of becoming anything', yet she too is now transformed into something very different. Could it also not be said that she is treated by the family as something of a convenience? She is certainly used as a convenience by her aunt, Lady Bertram. And in three years' time they will all most certainly be forgetting what she was before! Tellingly, Mary Crawford fails to hear these remarks or those that follow, thus reinforcing once again the ornamental nature of Fanny's role at Mansfield.

There are many other parts of the book which can be seen as having a symbolic as well as a literal value. Think of the sections of the book which deal with the subject of 'improving'. This was a popular enterprise in the eighteenth century and many estates were 'improved' by the likes of Capability Brown (1715–83) and Humphrey Repton (1752–1818). And yet, as Alistair Duckworth shows in *The Improvement of the Estate* (1971, Johns Hopkins University Press, revised 1994) the process of improving has another meaning, too, within *Mansfield Park*. Alistair Duckworth suggests that the estate in Austen's novels is symbolic of an inherited culture (see pp. 60–61, in the chapter 'Modern critical approaches'). Fanny is taken to Mansfield Park to be *improved*. The Crawfords try to bring their more cosmopolitan view of the world to Mansfield with the hope of *improving* it. Yet another example of Austen's symbolism can be found in the scene in the woods at Sotherton when Fanny is deserted by the others. You might like to think about the ways in which what happens there prefigures what happens in the main story.

The play *Lovers' Vows*

The most complex and most discussed aspect of the symbolism in *Mansfield Park* is contained within the theatrical rehearsals in the first part of the book. There are many aspects of the whole affair which pre-figure and mirror events which occur later in the novel. Take, for example, the roles played by each character in the play:

Maria	Agatha Friburg	A street beggar, once a chambermaid and mother of Fredrick.
Henry	Fredrick	Illegitimate and long-lost son of Agatha.
Mr Yates	Baron Wildenhaim	Seducer of Agatha, father of Fredrick. Now a wealthy landowner and widower.
Mary	Amelia	Daughter of the baron and very much in love with Anhalt.
Edmund	Anhalt	Tutor to Amelia; a vicar who is the spiritual adviser to the Baron.
Mr Rushworth	Count Cassel	A very stupid and rich fop who Amelia is to marry.
Tom and Mrs Grant/Fanny	Cottagers	They give shelter to Agatha and her son.

The parallels between their roles in *Lovers' Vows* and the roles they play in the action of the novel are striking. Most obviously, Rushworth is typecast as the stupid but rich Count Cassel. Amelia is in love with Anhalt and, similarly, there is an attraction between the two actors in these roles: Mary Crawford and Edmund. The choice of roles for Yates is also apt, given his actions later in the novel.

Yet it is not just the inadvisability of the roles within the play that lies at the heart of the opposition felt by Edmund and Fanny. The play itself would have been seen by contemporary readers as a somewhat scurrilous drama, one that certainly advocated a moral stance which opposed traditional moralities of marriage and fidelity. It was also felt inappropriate that Maria, as a woman engaged to be married, should enact scenes of some passion with Henry. Whilst it is this sense of propriety that it is difficult for modern readers to understand, it can certainly be said that, given later events, the judgements of Edmund and Fanny are shown to be correct.

The moral standpoint of the novel is provided throughout by the voices of Edmund and Fanny. Fanny, in particular, is disapproving of everything that contradicts what seems to be her natural evaluation of what is right and proper. The Crawfords and their desire for improvement, the Bertrams and their moral ambivalence, the petty perniciousness of Mrs Norris and even the social limitations of her own family are all subject to Fanny's disapproval. The end of the novel shows her judgement to be correct.

EMMA

Emma is regarded by many critics as the first great English novel. Hidden beneath what can appear to be a very simple plot there lies an intricate and complex structure which reaches well beyond the '3 or 4 characters in a Country Village', as Jane Austen was later to characterize her work.

The opening of the novel

The novel opens with a description of the **eponymous** heroine:

> Emma Woodhouse, handsome, clever, and rich, with a comfortable home and happy disposition, seemed to unite some of the best blessings of existence; and had lived nearly twenty-one years in the world with very little to distress or vex her.

KEYWORD

An **eponymous** hero or heroine is one whose name appears in the title of the work, for example, *Don Juan*, *Robinson Crusoe*, *Tess of the d'Urbervilles*.

This appears to be a piece of wholesome praise: here is a secure young woman who is all that could be wished for and who has all she requires. Yet Austen in planning Emma wrote, 'I am going to take a heroine whom no one but myself will much like' (cited in Austen-Leigh, J. E., *A Memoir of Jane Austen* now published with *Persuasion* in Penguin Classics, p. 376). There are hints in this opening paragraph that all might not be quite as it seems, but they are subtle ones. Notice that word 'seemed' in the middle of the sentence. It suggests the privileging of appearance over reality; Emma only 'seemed' to 'unite some of the best blessings of existence'. And as we read on we realize this is indeed a novel about perceptions. What *seems* to be obvious to Emma is often not the case at all, merely her over-fertile imagination muddling her judgement. Look, too, at the second part of the opening sentence. On the one hand it suggests innocence, even naivety, but there is also the suggestion that she has been over-protected, spoilt even. This is a theme which is continued in the opening four paragraphs as evidenced by the ironic comments on Emma's independence and the lack of restraints on her behaviour.

The story, then, is that of Emma Woodhouse, who may be 'handsome, clever and rich', yet lacks many of the usual accomplishments that so often define femininity in the Austen novel. Emma is without the musical and artistic talents to adequately amuse herself. Her apparent defining interest lies in her role as matchmaker. Having successfully married (and hence lost) her governess to Mr Weston she seeks now to find a suitable match for her new protégée, Harriet Smith. Undeterred by both Miss Smith's illegitimacy and lack of wealth, she seeks to match her first with the vicar, Mr Elton, and next with the spirited Frank Churchill, whilst at the same time to dissuade Harriet from the more lowly born, yet far more suitable, Robert Martin. Such manipulations are destined to failure and we observe Emma's distress and embarrassment as her plans fall, one by one, into total disarray. Meantime, unbeknown to Emma, her own resolution to remain single becomes less and less tenable.

Subjectivity

Emma is the primary centre of consciousness within the novel; we see much that takes place through her eyes, having frequent access to her thoughts and perceptions of the world around her. Austen's use of free indirect discourse means that the story is often told from Emma's perspective. The narration, rather than being an objective appraisal of the story, can mislead the reader, particularly when the narrator's viewpoint and that of Emma's begin to merge (see Chapter 2 for an example of this). This technique can be seen as an early example of the use of the **fallible** or **unreliable narrator**.

Emma's assessment of the world around her is continually shown to be driven by her own fertile imagination and ours, too, as readers of the narrative can be similarly misled. As we read the novel and begin to understand Emma's tendency to see things incorrectly, so we find ourselves questioning her judgement, wondering whether what we are being shown by the narrator is what is real or yet again misjudged.

> **KEYWORD**
>
> Fallible or unreliable narrator: This is often used in novels written in the first person to mislead the reader by presenting something about which the narrator is mistaken as a seeming truth. *The Catcher in the Rye* and *The Great Gatsby* are obvious modern examples. Austen narrates her novels in the third person but her (again early) use of free indirect discourse means that the viewpoint of the narrator and that of the heroine are often difficult to separate.

This is made explicit in the novel by Emma's continual misreading of the romantic inclinations of her acquaintances. She supposes that Mr Elton, the vicar of Highbury, is in love with Harriet and so encourages her to fall in love with him. In the following extract Mr Elton has been encouraged by Emma to contribute a riddle to Harriet's collection. He produces one, claiming it to be written by a friend:

> 'I do not offer it for Miss Smith's collection,' said he. 'Being my friend's, I have no right to expose it in any degree to the public eye, but perhaps you may not dislike looking at it.'

The speech was more to Emma than to Harriet, which Emma could understand. There was deep consciousness about him, and he found it easier to meet her eye than her friend's. He was gone the next moment: – after another moment's pause,

'Take it,' said Emma, smiling, and pushing the paper towards Harriet – 'it is for you. Take your own.'

(*Emma*, Volume 1, Chapter 9)

First, notice here how the narrative voice is reflecting Emma's perception. The middle paragraph of the extract above shows Emma's view of events, not that of an objective narrator. Second, look at what it is that Emma sees. We are told that Emma could understand that he found it easier to address her than her friend. She attributes this to a 'deep consciousness'. Yet we, as readers, are not fooled into believing this to be true. In this we are attuned to Austen's ironic style of narration. We begin to suspect that it is not a deep sensitivity which forces Elton to address his words to Emma rather than Harriet but that Emma (and the narrator) has got it totally wrong! It is not her friend who is being courted but Emma herself. As Emma proceeds to advance Mr Elton's cause to Harriet we can observe, with some amusement, the weaknesses of her judgement. It is not until Elton drunkenly makes direct advances to Emma that she realizes the error of her ways and how terribly she has deceived not just herself but also her friend.

Emma and puzzles

Emma has often been compared to a detective story with the reader, like Emma herself, in the role of detective trying to work out what exactly is going on, particularly in terms of the Frank Churchill/Jane Fairfax mystery. J. M. Q. Davies, in his essay on *Emma*, takes this argument a stage further, suggesting that the whole idea of puzzles and their solution is central to our reading of the novel. He suggests that in *Emma*, Austen is playing a game with her readers, a game that has both a serious and a humorous purpose. In this game Austen is teasing her readers, presenting them with literal conundrums such as Mr Elton's riddle but also those more subtle riddles contained within the structure of the novel itself. Her purpose is:

> … to tease readers into the realisation that they too are participating in a sophisticated fictional game. It is a game in which the charade on courtship, the entire Elton episode and the main Jane Fairfax–Frank Churchill mystery are related rather like a set of Chinese boxes, each confronting the reader with successively more complex puzzles.
>
> (Davies, J.M.Q., 'Emma' as Charade and the Education of the Reader,
> *Philological Quarterly*, 65 (1986) reprinted in *New Casebooks: Emma*,
> Monaghan, D. (ed.), 1992, Macmillan, pp. 80–81)

The humorous purpose is, of course, that of entertainment. The serious purpose Davies suggests is educative aimed particularly at younger readers and designed to sharpen their powers of judgement. He points particularly to the game of charades in Volume 1, Chapter 9, suggesting it functions as a key to reading the text. Whilst Emma can easily solve the charade puzzle contained in Mr Elton's poem, she is as inept as Harriet in deciphering the language of Elton's courtship. Davies sees the novel as presenting a whole series of such tests for Emma to perform and that it is only after developing the ability to solve these that she is able to deal effectively with life. The reader, too, is led along a similar path gaining in experience as they solve the complexities of the novel's structure.

Mr Knightley

If Emma is seen as one of Austen's fallible heroines who undertakes a journey towards enlightenment through the course of the novel, then Knightley is often seen as one of Austen's wise and resolute male heroes. Men in Austen's novels are often shadowy figures whose lives, away from the courtship plots, seem to lack definition. Mr Bennet in *Pride and Prejudice*, for example, simply disappears conveniently into the library when his presence is not required in the lives of his wife and daughters. Knightley, though, is shown to be a man who does exist beyond Hartwell, actively managing his farm, taking note and regard of his responsibilities.

Many have found him to be the voice of reason and rationality, what Alistair Duckworth calls the 'normative and exemplary figure' (*The Improvement of the Estate*, p. 148). Certainly he warns Emma against interfering in the lives of others, disapproves of her attempts at matchmaking, dislikes the flighty behaviour of Frank Churchill and admonishes Emma severely for her rudeness to Miss Bates at Box Hill. He asks her:

> 'How could you be so unfeeling to Miss Bates? How could you be so insolent in your wit to a woman of her character, age, and situation? – Emma, I had not thought it possible.'
>
> (*Emma*, Volume 3, Chapter 7)

It is as severe an attack upon a heroine as any other in Austen's novels and the mortification Emma suffers is equal only to that felt by Elizabeth in *Pride and Prejudice* after she reads Darcy's letter. As a moment of signification in the narrative it serves the same purpose as Darcy's letter, marking the start of Emma's reformation. Her shame at her actions and regret at parting from Knightley without thanking him for his honesty are feelings that remain with Emma as moments of revelation. It leads the way to that next moment of revelation:

> It darted through her, with the speed of an arrow, that Mr Knightley must marry no one but herself!
>
> (*Emma*, Volume 3, Chapter 11)

Whilst suddenly acknowledging her feelings comes as a surprise to Emma, the reader has been consciously, if subtly prepared. Look, for example, at the end of Volume 1, Chapter 5 where it is clear that the marriage of Knightley and Emma has been seen by the Weston's as desirable for a very long time.

Yet there is a sense that the novel, from the outset, has been about preparing Emma for her marriage. At one level this can be seen as a novel about the process of growing up. It seems that, in order to marry Mr Knightley, Emma has to learn to become less subjective and to recognize her own limitations. We, as readers, have the opportunity to make the same discovery for ourselves.

PERSUASION

Like all of Jane Austen's heroines, except Emma Woodhouse, Anne Elliot is a woman of limited means who will ultimately be rescued from the dire threat of even further reduced circumstances and spinsterhood by a 'fortunate' marriage. *Persuasion* is Austen's most mature novel and in tone and style certainly is markedly different from the other five novels. Perhaps in *Persuasion* we have a sense of how Austen would have developed as a writer had she not died so prematurely.

The story is, as the title suggests, a tale of gradual and eventual persuasion. Anne Elliott's refusal of Wentworth some eight years previously on the advice of her trusted friend Lady Russell is now viewed by her with considerable regret. When Wentworth, now a wealthy Captain in the Royal Navy, returns it seems at first that he is more attracted by Anne's cousins Louisa and Henrietta, particularly the former. A terrible accident occurs at Lyme Regis which leaves Louisa injured. At this time Wentworth begins once again to be attracted to Anne. Louisa's subsequent engagement to another naval officer, Captain Benwick, frees Wentworth to pursue Anne to Bath. Here it seems that Anne has another suitor, her cousin, and the heir to her former home, Kellynch Hall, William Elliot. The unmasking of Elliot as an unmitigated bounder and the discovery by Wentworth that Anne still loves him leads to the almost inevitable Austen ending.

Anne Elliot

Anne Elliot is considerably older than any of Austen's other heroines and certainly at the start of the book would seem to be destined for that most dreaded state, an unhappy spinsterhood. We are told:

A few years before, Anne Elliot had been a very pretty girl, but her bloom
had vanished early; and as even in its height, her father had found little
to admire in her, (so totally different were her delicate features and mild
dark eyes from his own), there could be nothing in them, now that she
was faded and thin, to excite his esteem.

(*Persuasion*, Chapter 1)

Later in the same chapter she is described even more brutally as
'haggard'. No wonder then that at her first meeting for eight years with
Captain Wentworth she is told that she is, 'So altered that he should not
have known her again' (Chapter 1).

Both D. W. Harding in his introduction to the Penguin edition of
Persuasion and Cheryl Ann Weissman comment on the similarity
between this novel and the fairytale story of Cinderella. Here we have

the villainous and unloving parent, the two selfish sisters, a well-intentioned if misguided godmother in the form of Lady Russell with the rich Prince Charming role played by Captain Wentworth. Yet as Harding notes, Anne Elliot is a much more mature and more complex character than the 'real' Cinderella. She has contrived to cause her own unhappiness by her previous decision to reject Wentworth's proposal of marriage. There is also, as Weissman notes, the irony provided by the appearance of a second suitor:

> With fairy tale symmetry, Anne could … be restored to her home and in some measure be compensated for the wrongs done her by a godmother's error in judgement and a natural mother's symbolic abandonment. We, as readers, can see that the legacy also includes her mother's terrible folly of marrying an unworthy man …
>
> (Weissman, C. A., 'Doubleness and Refrain in *Persuasion*', *The Kenyon Review*, 10:4 (1988) reprinted in Simmons, J., *New Casebook: Mansfield Park and Persuasion*, 1997, Macmillan, p. 206)

What we seem to have in Anne Elliot is similar to the Cinderella myth in yet one more respect. There is within her a potential simply waiting for the right moment to emerge. The transformation seems suddenly to take effect during the calamitous visit to Lyme Regis.

The moment of change for Anne, the moment when she begins to once again attract the attentions of both Captain Wentworth and his rival Sir Walter Elliot is also marked by a change in her appearance:

> Anne's face caught his eye, and he looked at her with a degree of earnest admiration, which she could not be insensible of. She was looking remarkably well; her very regular, very pretty features, having the bloom and freshness of youth restored by the fine wind which had been blowing on her complexion, and by the animation of eye which it had also produced.
>
> (*Persuasion*, Chapter 12)

Unnoticed by her father or her sisters, acknowledged but untapped by Lady Russell, it takes a near fatal accident her metamorphosis to begin.

The accident

The moment when Louisa falls from the steps on the Cobb at Lyme Regis seems a decisive one in Anne's fate. It is a moment when all eyes turn to her and as she is held as the subject of everyone's gaze there comes about a transformation. Not only does Anne take command, but it seems that no action is possible without her edict. As Louisa lies 'lifeless' on the pavement Mary cries, 'She is dead! She is dead!' and grips Charles in such a way as 'to make him immovable'. At the same time Henrietta faints. Wentworth turns pale 'in an agony of silence' only managing to ask for help 'in a tone of despair, and as if all his strength were gone'. Only Anne manages to keep her head. She orders Captain Benwick to assist Wentworth and then immediately prescribes a range of medical aid, 'Rub her hands, rub her temple; here are salts, – take them, take them.' The narrator tells us, 'everything was done that Anne prompted.' As none of this has any effect and Wentworth staggers against the wall he can think only of the effect upon Louisa's parents. It is again left to Anne to prompt the next action. She orders a surgeon and then as Wentworth begins to obey her command she stops him and substitutes Benwick. As he runs for help, Anne is left to comfort and support the remaining members of the party. Notice here how all look to Anne for what they require:

> Anne, attending with all the strength and zeal, and thought, which instinct supplied, to Henrietta, still tried, at intervals, to suggest comfort to the others, tried to quiet Mary, to animate Charles, to assuage the feelings of Captain Wentworth. Both seemed to look to her for directions.
>
> (*Persuasion*, Chapter 12)

Both Charles and Wentworth now apply to her for their next actions:

> 'Anne, Anne,' cried Charles, 'What is to be done next? What, in heaven's name, is to be done next?'
> Captain Wentworth's eyes were also turned towards her.

Anne becomes the centre of the action – a heroine of the moment and it marks a turning point in her renewed relationship with Captain Wentworth. When they next meet in Bath some time later it is he who is seen to blush and Anne who feels for the first time that she 'had the advantage of him' (Chapter 19).

The ending

Austen was unhappy with way she originally drew the threads of her story together and as a consequence rewrote the penultimate chapter, substituting two new chapters in its place. Certainly the scene at the White Hart Inn provides a most effective climax to the relationship between Anne and Captain Wentworth, Anne's philosophical discussion of fidelity and constancy with Captain Harville contrasts sharply with the urgency and strength of Wentworth's letter. And to use Austen's phraseology: 'Who can be in doubt of what followed?' (*Persuasion*, Chapter 24). As one of the Butler-defined 'heroines who are right', the change that is effected in Anne would seem to be more one of recognition than of substance. When Wentworth tells her at the end of the novel 'to my eye you were never altered' (Chapter 23), we can see this (as does Anne herself) as rather dubious flattery. Wentworth himself has changed at least in fortune and this is enough to persuade Sir Walter Elliot that the eventual marriage should be entered into his favourite volume.

✳ ✳ ✳ *SUMMARY* ✳ ✳ ✳

● *Mansfield Park* is Austen's most difficult and most complex novel. It can be seen as an exploration of the difference between appearance and reality.

● *Emma* is a novel which explores the problems of subjectivity.

● *Persuasion* is Austen's most mature novel.

Early critical approaches

7

Jane Austen achieved a modest critical success in her own lifetime. For example, she received a very favourable review of *Emma* from the man who was the most popular literary figure of the time, Sir Walter Scott. Sir Walter further remarked in his notebook:

> That young lady had a talent for describing the involvement and feelings and characters of ordinary life which is to me the most wonderful I ever met with. The Big Bow-wow strain I can do myself like any now going, but the exquisite touch which renders ordinary commonplace things and characters interesting from the truth of the description and the sentiment is denied to me. What a pity such a gifted creature died so early!
>
> (Tait, J. G. (ed.) *Journal of Walter Scott*, entry for 14 March 1826)

Scott's distinction here between the 'Big Bow-wow strain' and Austen's concern for the 'ordinary commonplace thing' is an observance which seems to have been made down the centuries. For Scott, the difference is between his large-scale dramas of war, power and history painted on a huge canvas and Austen's concern for life in the drawing-rooms of a small segment of Regency society. Richard Whately, writing in 1821 on the publication of *Emma*, concerns himself with the moral lessons to be learned from reading the novel and concludes:

> On the whole, Miss Austen's works may be safely recommended, not only as among the most unexceptionable of their class, but as combining, in an eminent degree, instruction with amusement, though without the direct effort at the former, of which we have complained, as sometimes defeating its object.
>
> (From *Quarterly Review* XXIV, January 1821)

He judges it as entertainment rather than as instructional reading and concludes that as such, Austen may be thanked for it is better to read this than some other piece which may not be as innocent. This would seem to be very much in keeping with an essentially eighteenth-century concern with novel reading as an educational experience rather than as mere entertainment.

The novels were also popular with the Prince Regent who kept a full set in each of his residences and who also invited Austen to dedicate *Emma* to himself.

George Lewes suggested that Austen was a 'prose Shakespeare' (reprinted in Southam, B., *Jane Austen: The Critical Heritage Volume 1*, 1987, Routledge & Kegan Paul, No. 27), although he later qualified this and suggested that it was only 'plenitude of power' which saved her from being both tedious and commonplace (*ibid.*, No. 30).

Yet after Austen's death in 1817 she seems to have faded from both public acclaim and critical interest. It was not until the publication of J. E. Austen-Leigh's memoir of his aunt in 1870 that interest again began to grow in the author and her works. The period is an

> **KEYWORD**
>
> Canon: The body of writing that is accepted as representative of a period or a culture.

interesting moment in the history of English literature for it was a time when the so called **canon** of English literature was being very consciously constructed. This canon was more than just a list of good works, it also had a serious moral and social purpose. An account of this rise can be found in Chapter 1 of Terry Eagleton's *Literary Theory: An Introduction* (1996, Blackwell). Yet not all critical acclaim for Austen was wholly positive. Ralph Emerson, the American philosopher and poet, wrote in his journal:

> I am at a loss to understand why people hold Miss Austen's novels at so high a rate, which seem to me vulgar in tone, sterile in artistic invention, imprisoned in the wretched conventions of English society without genius, wit or knowledge of the world.
>
> (Quoted in Southam, op. cit., p 28)

Henry James, too, was hardly complimentary, seeing the genius of Austen's writing as something accidental rather than consciously purposeful. In what must be one of the longest, most condescending and rambling critical comments in the history of criticism, he writes:

> The key to Jane Austen's fortune with posterity has been in part the extraordinary grace of her facility, in fact of her unconsciousness: as if, at the most, for difficulty, for embarrassment, she sometimes, over her work basket, her tapestry flowers, in the spare cool, drawing room of other days, fell-a-musing, lapsed too metaphorically, as one may say, onto wool-gathering, and her dropped stitches, of these pardonable, of these precious moments, were afterwards picked up as little touches of human truth, little glimpses of steady vision, little master-strokes of imagination.
>
> (Taken from Southam, B., *Jane Austen: The Critical Heritage, Volume 2 1870 –1940*, 1987, Routledge & Kegan Paul, p. 229)

F. R. Leavis declared in his opening sentence of his seminal work, *The Great Tradition*:

> The great English novelists are Jane Austen, George Eliot, Henry James and Joseph Conrad ...
>
> (1948, Chatto and Windus)

He went on to conclude that Austen was so great that she deserved a work of her own in which to establish this greatness, a task he never quite got around to. His wife Q. D. Leavis did write an article in their flagship magazine *Scrutiny* which looked at Austen's process of writing. In this she argues that each novel went through a rigorous process of drafting and puts forward the theory that the sources of the great novels could be found in early more minor works. She sees the novels as 'geological structures' and Austen as a 'steady professional writer who had to put in many years of labour and thought to achieve each novel' (*Scrutiny*, Vol X, 1941).

By the mid-twentieth century Austen was established as one of the 'greats'. Her works were studied on university courses and became set texts for GCE and GCSE exam boards. There was still a tendency to see Austen as a writer who ignored (either wilfully or through ignorance) the affairs of the world. Her novels, with their narrowly defined horizons and domestic plots, seemed to have little to do with the wars and revolutions, the social changes and political turmoils of the late eighteenth and early nineteenth centuries. Such views were about to be blasted away.

✳ ✳ ✳SUMMARY✳ ✳ ✳

● Austen achieved a modest degree of success in her own lifetime.

● The majority of nineteenth-century writers and critics recognized her greatness.

● A number of others criticized her for the smallness of her vision.

● By the mid-twentieth century she was established as part of the canon of English literature.

Modern critical approaches

8

MARILYN BUTLER

Two works more than any others marked the development of Austen criticism in the 1970s and continue to play an important role until this day. The first of these was Marilyn Butler's *Jane Austen and the War of Ideas* (1975, OUP). It is one of those pieces of critical writing which fundamentally alter the way we read an author. Up to this point Austen had been seen largely as a writer who created worlds curiously unconnected with the political and social events of her time. Austen's (probably ironical) comment that she created a world defined as 'the little bits (two inches wide) of ivory on which I work with so fine a brush, as produces little effect after much labour' (Letter date 16 December, 1816) had been over-interpreted.

Butler showed Austen to be a writer who was very much involved in the ideological debates of her time. She shows Austen to be both a Christian moralist and a conservative thinker opposed to the political revolutionary **Jacobin** movement that was sweeping across Europe. As such, she recreates Jane Austen as a wholly different writer from the one that existed for the previous generation. To illustrate her viewpoint here is a summary of part of her interpretation of *Mansfield Park*.

> ### KEYWORD
>
> **Jacobin:** A term derived from the French Revolution. The Jacobins were a French political society established in 1789 at the old Dominican convent in Paris. The term as used by Butler and elsewhere is usually synonymous with 'revolutionary'.

Butler's view of *Mansfield Park*

Butler sees *Mansfield Park*, like a number of other novels of the period, to be formulated around the issue of girls' education. The Bertram girls are shown to be shallow, vain and self-seeking. Fanny, in contrast, is a Christian who possesses the very qualities the Bertram girls lack:

Jane Austen was opposed to the revolutionary movements taking place across Europe.

humility together with awareness of both her own failings and of the need for external guidance. These Butler sees as explicitly Christian values. The contrast between Fanny and the Bertrams is heightened by the arrival of the Crawfords. Their sophisticated, materialistic, consciously self-seeking and self-patronizing attitudes set up what Butler calls a 'triple contrast'. Every early scene is presented by reference to the education and moral attitudes of the three sets of protagonists: Fanny/Edmund, Maria/Julia and Mary/Henry.

Butler identifies three issues which are explored within the novel that allow Austen to present, through Fanny and Edmund, a clear Christian and anti-Jacobin position. These issues are nature, religion and marriage. She cites the visit to Sotherton as an occasion upon which the ideological issues come to the fore. Fanny, in particular, takes a definite stance on nature, preferring rural life as it provides a structured environment in which the individual's place and duty to the community is well defined.

Butler comments:

> Sotherton is, or ought to be, a Burkean, symbol of human lives led among natural surroundings, man contiguous with nature and continuous with his own past. Fanny finds it both these things.
>
> (Butler, M., *Jane Austen and the War of Ideas*, 1975, OUP, p. 225)

The Crawfords, in contrast, use the visit to propose 'improving' Sotherton, that is to change and thereby destroy the existing landscape of the estate.

Secondly, on the subject of religion, a huge gap appears at Sotherton between the Fanny/Edmund position and that of the Crawfords – the former identifying a spiritual and social dimension to orthodox Christianity and the latter, Mary in particular, expressing a complete indifference. The contrast here is between Mary's self-serving individualism and a care and concern for both others and established religious convention, as Fanny's comment on family worship shows:

> 'It is a pity,' cried Fanny, 'that the custom should have been discontinued. It was a valuable part of former times. There is something in a chapel and chaplain so much in character with a great house, with one's ideas of what such a household should be! A whole family assembling regularly for the purpose of prayer is fine!'
>
> (*Mansfield Park*, Chapter 9)

Thirdly, the theme of marriage is also shown to be an ideological battleground. This is explored in relation to Maria's intended marriage to Rushworth. There are first the hollow references to the marriage within the chapel itself and then the enactment within the woods mimetic of so much that is about to occur in the next section of the novel. This theme is also, of course, further explored in the rehearsal for the play *Lovers' Vows* (see Chapter 6).

Butler believes there to be a clear and explicit relationship between action and thought within the novel:

The action of the novel is so entirely bound up with the value systems of the various characters that they are always to a greater or lesser extent illustrating, acting out, their beliefs.

(Butler, ibid., p. 227)

ALISTAIR DUCKWORTH

The second work of criticism which has been key in redefining our understanding of Austen is Alistair Duckworth's *The Improvement of the Estate*, originally published in 1971 but revised in 1994. Duckworth, too, stressed the political position Austen takes in her novels, seeing her, as does Butler, as a conservative. The estate for Duckworth acts as much more than mere bricks and mortar. It symbolizes a contained and harmonious world, a world that has evolved through many succeeding and successful generations. This world incorporates not just the rules of how to behave but more a whole way of being. The estate is the inheritance of both a sense of self and the relative position of that self in a structured and secure world. One example of this is the relationship between owners and their estates in the novels:

> Throughout Jane Austen's fiction, estates function not only as the settings of action but as indexes to the character and social responsibility of the owners.

(Duckworth, A., The Improvement of the Estate, 1994,
Johns Hopkins University Press, p. 38)

Thus, the 'aesthetic good sense' apparent in the landscape at Pemberley is a reflection of Darcy's good character, similarly the description of Donwell Abbey in Volume 3, Chapter 6 of *Emma* can also be seen as a comment on Knightley's stewardship. In contrast, Sir Walter Elliot in abandoning his duty and renting out Kellynch Hall in *Persuasion* and the landscape improvements in *Mansfield Park* can be seen as indictments of their owners. For Duckworth this 'recurring motif' allows Austen to comment (largely negatively) on the process of social change. For Duckworth, then, the estate has both a literal function and a symbolic one.

As Duckworth acknowledges in his 1994 preface to the paperback edition, it was too early a work to have been much influenced by the new forces of criticism which were just beginning to make their appearance.

STRUCTURALISM AND POST-STRUCTURALISM

There was a significant change in the focus of literary criticism which developed in the late 1960s and on into the 1970s. This was first marked by the emergence of an approach known as **Structuralism**. Structuralism began with the work of Claude Lévi Strauss and Roland Barthes. As the name suggests, it is concerned with structures and the notion that these structures can exist only in relation to one another. In essence, using the ideas of Swiss linguist Ferdinand de Saussure, structuralists stress the arbitrary nature of language.

The changes that Structuralism brought to the world of literary criticism more or less bypassed the novels of Jane Austen until well into the 1980s. By this time the cultural revolution in literary criticism had moved along apace and **post-structuralist** approaches had gained the upper hand. These were based on the work of another broad range of French philosophers, foremost amongst them Jacques Derrida. Derrida took the ideas of the structuralists a stage or two further. He argued that if it is language which structures our world rather than a clear and definite reality then

KEYWORDS

Structuralism: A movement which emphasized the functions of language and the patterns found within it. Language is seen as a self-contained system of signs in which meaning is found in the fact that one sign is different from another. So the word 'door' is different from the word 'window', but both are seen as arbitrary labels for things in the world.

Post-structuralism: The term is often used synonymously with deconstructionism, a movement led by Jacques Derrida, Roland Barthes, the post-Freudian analysts Jacques Lacan and Julia Kristeva and the historical critiques of Michael Foucault amongst others. It argues for what is called the instability of meanings where there are no fixed points, no absolutes and no hierarchies but rather a lot of uncertainty and what is called plurality or free play. It rejects the idea of there being an intrinsic meaning within a text which can be extracted by means of careful analysis.

there are no beginnings and no ends which are not in some way
structured by language. In simple terms there is no reality outside the
construction of language. Post-structuralist criticism suggests that there
is no absolute way to read a text and so refutes the highly conservative
interpretations of Austen which had existed before the 1970s.

One task which post-structuralist critics frequently undertake is to
explore the gaps within a narrative, to look at those elements within a
novel which seem to lie just beyond the reach of the narrator's vision.
Angela Leighton, for example, looks at the silences, at what is *not* said,
in *Sense and Sensibility*. Her interest is particularly focused on
Marianne, whose voice, thoughts and feelings are, as the novel
progresses, heard only through the rationality of her sister's
observations. Meanwhile, of course, Elinor is also struggling to remain
silent, both to keep Marianne's secret and to protect others from her
own distress. Leighton sees an important difference in the silences of
the two sisters:

> … the Silences of Elinor are those of reserve and integrity; the Silences
> of Marianne are those of nonconformity and emotional powerlessness.
> (Leighton, A., *Jane Austen: New Perspectives* (New York, 1983) reprinted
> in *New Casebooks: Sense and Sensibility and Pride and Prejudice*,
> Clark, R. (ed.) 1994, Macmillan, p. 56)

Elinor's silences though 'have Austen's approval' and are included as
part of the narrative. We see the reasons for Elinor's silence and we also
know, through the narrative, what it contains.

Jill Heydt-Stevenson also takes a post-
structuralist approach. In her essay '"Slipping
into the Ha-Ha": Bawdy Humour and the Body
Politics in Jane Austen's Novels' *(Nineteenth
Century Literature*, Vol. 5, No. 3, December
2000) she reminds us that words are **signs** but
what they signify, what they represent, is not
always clear. The language in Austen's text does

KEYWORD

A **signifer** or a **sign** is a
label which suggests a
signified or an object in
the real world. For
example, the sign
created by the three
letters 'c – o – w' suggests
a four-legged beast
which chews grass and
produces milk.

not mean merely what it seems to mean at the surface level. She suggests a number of meanings that transgress the apparent and points to a playfulness in Austen's language. She further suggests that Austen is far more consciously aware of the sexual innuendoes contained within her text than has been generally allowed.

She challenges the readings of Austen in which sexuality is curiously suppressed and in doing so uncovers a surprising range of bawdy humour. She first reminds us of Mary Crawford's unambiguously crude remark in *Mansfield Park*:

> Certainly, my home at my uncle's brought me acquainted with a circle of admirals. Of Rears and Vices I saw enough. Now do not be suspecting me of a pun, I entreat.
>
> (*Mansfield Park*, Chapter 6)

Mary's reference here to sodomy is unavoidable. Heydt-Stevenson argues, that once we admit to this and allow for a bawdy humour in the novels then we can begin to explore further. The riddle half-remembered by Mr Woodhouse in *Emma*, for example, is in fact about a man suffering from venereal disease. As for *Mansfield Park*, Heydt-Stevenson sees it as positively libidinous!

> The general content is inescapably erotic: the characters openly canvas Fanny's developing body, and Austen herself offers a worldly and unfazed description of the crime of adultery, which contrasts comically to Fanny's scandalized descriptions of it.
>
> (*Nineteenth Century Literature*, Vol. 5, No. 3, p. 324)

Heydt-Stevenson's argument rests upon a close study of the text, which again suggests a post-structuralist reading. She looks particularly at the tendency of language to suggest more than one reading (one signifier and many signifieds). She notes, for example, that nearly every character in the novel is trying to 'make' or 'be made'. The verb suggests both promotion but also (then as today) has sexual connotations. Fanny's name, too, had the same colloquial connotations in the early

1900s as it does today, particularly as John Cleland's *Memoirs of a Woman of Pleasure* (1749) had only recently introduced both the prostitute Fanny Hill and the slang term 'fanny'. She finds many examples where Austen's language implies, or at least allows for, a sexualized reading. Lady Russell's appreciation of Wentworth's manhood and Elinor and Mrs Dashwood's appreciation of Willoughby's are two examples the reader may wish to explore. In taking this view, though, Heydt-Stevenson is not just raking the dirt. She argues very persuasively that Austen deliberately and consciously uses bawdy humour to subvert and attack those patriarchal ideologies which operated to keep women in a subservient social and economic position.

'The handsomest and best hung of any in Bath.'

For another example of post-structuralist criticism, see references to the essay by J. M. Q. Davies on *Emma* in Chapter 6. Also of interest is D. A. Miller's *Narrative and its Discontents: Problems of Closure in the Traditional Novel* (1981, Princeton). As the title suggests this looks at the tension that exists between the language of the novel, with all its slippery inconclusiveness, and the need to use this language to reach the happy endings required of the traditional novel. It is by no means an easy read but is a very good example of post-structuralism at work.

FEMINIST APPROACHES TO AUSTEN

In exploring issues related to the silencing of women in narratives, Leighton is in the company of many **feminist** writers and academics who explore literature from a female perspective.

Feminist criticism is a diverse and eclectic field of study. Its origins can be traced back to the women's movements of the 1960s, and beyond. Early feminist criticism was polemical and combative, fighting against a dominant ideology that placed men hierarchically above women.

Gilbert and Gubar

As novels both written by a women and concerned almost exclusively with the affairs of women, Jane Austen's work has been of obvious attraction to feminist criticism. One of the foremost works in this area is the extensive study of nineteenth-century women's writing, *The Madwoman in the Attic* by Sandra Gilbert and Susan Gubar (1979). It is an example of what has come to be termed **gynocriticism**.

> ## KEYWORDS
>
> **Feminism:** The study of gender politics from a female perspective. Usually the term is applied to the political and social movement which swept Western Europe and the United States beginning in the late 1960s.
>
> **Gynocriticsm:** This focuses on women writers in an attempt to challenge traditionally male-defined (and male-dominated) literary canon. It looks at what defines and distinguishes female writing from its male counterpart.

Gilbert and Gubar see the whole concept of literary authority in Western culture as exclusively male and ask the question: where does this leave women writers? Not only have women been excluded from authorship but they have also become the 'subjects to (and subjects of) male authority' (p. 11). They are reduced to characters seen as 'mere properties' imprisoned within male texts. Women denied 'authorship' instead can become only objects of male representation. Where, then, does this leave Jane Austen?

One way they suggest that Austen was able to write from within such a male-dominated culture was by defining a small space separate from the world at large (it's that little bit of ivory again). Austen, they argue, admits and accepts the discomforts of a patriarchal culture yet manages to both use and subvert the limitations that it imposes. One way this is achieved is through Austen's use of what they characterize as a duplicitous female language. This appears to be docile and restrained but is actually at the same time assertive and rebellious. Austen's ironic narratorial voice is frequently found to be expressing a view that opposes a superficial reading of the text. The over-hasty conclusions to the novels with their unlikely coincidences is another example of this undercutting:

> … the implication remains that a girl without the aid of a benevolent narrator would never find a way out of either her mortifications or her parents' house. (op. cit., p. 169)

Another example of Austen duplicity is seen in the presentation of the powerful unpleasant women who play a small but significant role in each of the novels: Mrs Norris in *Mansfield Park*, Mrs Ferrars in *Sense and Sensibility* and Lady Catherine De Bourgh in *Pride and Prejudice* are just three examples. They see Mrs Norris as a 'dark parody' of Mary Crawford, her lively materialism degenerated into 'meddlesome, officious penny-pinching' (p. 170). Yet they also see her as a contrast to the ineffectual and passive Lady Bertram who does nothing all day but sit and stroke her pug. Lady Bertram, like other 'good' mothers in Austen's fiction epitomizes the necessity of submission if a woman is to successfully marry and achieve a life free from financial worries. Mrs Norris may be condemned to penury but not to submissive acquiescence. For Gilbert and Gubar, 'the figure of bad Aunt Norris implies that female strength, exertion, and passion are necessary for survival and pleasure' (p. 171). Similarly, the dreadful Catherine De Bourgh in *Pride and Prejudice* is seen in *Madwoman* as subverting the apparent meaning of the text. She is seen as very similar to Elizabeth Bennet (authoritative, judgemental, stubborn, courageous). Both are the only characters in the novel capable of expressing real anger. They both, too, share similar views. Lady Catherine's strong feelings about the unsuitability of Mrs Bennet only articulate Elizabeth's own thoughts; Lady Catherine's views on entailment cannot be different from Elizabeth's, given the restrictions it places on her and her sisters. Lady Catherine is a prime example of what Gilbert and Gubar term 'bitchy women' (p. 170) who act as doubles for both the heroines of the novel and for the author herself.

Gilbert and Gubar have been frequently criticized for the stance they take. For example, the way they privilege gender as opposed to class, religion or politics is seen as unnecessarily restrictive. Their dismissal of all women's writing earlier than Austen is seen as somewhat artificial. It has also been seen as an hysterical work particularly on account of its presentation of 'women's writing' as containing a single and unified value system which it patently did not.

KEYWORDS

Enlightenment: The philosophical movement that took place in Europe (particularly in France) in the eighteenth century in which reason and individualism were emphasized at the expense of tradition.

Mary Wollstonecraft (1759–97): Early radical fighter for women's rights and mother of Mary Shelley. Her most famous work was *A Vindication of the Rights of Women* published in 1792 which attacked the way in which women's education kept them passive and ignorant. It was most likely read by Austen and probably influenced *Mansfield Park*.

Margaret Kirkham

A different feminist viewpoint can be found in Margaret Kirkham's *Jane Austen, Feminism and Fiction*. She sees Austen as highly sympathetic to the rational feminism movement of the **Enlightenment**, particularly influenced by the controversial figure of **Mary Wollstonecraft**.

This detailed study is presented as a series of short essays each looking at an aspect of Austen's work as well as giving an overview of feminism and fiction in the period 1694–1798. Kirkham takes what is sometimes a controversial line. For example, she suggests that the portrayal of Fanny Price in *Mansfield Park* is an ironic one. She equates Fanny's saintliness with her ability to excite men's sexual passion:

Fanny's apparent innocence and religiosity is an aspect of her sexiness, a veneer of the 'angelic' which makes her sexually exciting to men like Crawford, who wish to find in their wives such vulnerable 'virtue' as well as excite both sexual passion and manly protectiveness.

(First published 1982, reprinted 1997 Athlone Press, p. 102)

Whilst Fanny may appear on the surface to be a highly conforming and conventional woman, Kirkham believes that discerning readers will see through this façade and see in Fanny a figure much more the fictionalized embodiment of Wollstonecraft's 'Enlightenment feminism'. For Fanny is ultimately shown to be strong, resolute and moreover morally right in her rejection of Henry Crawford. For Kirkham, Austen is an anti-Romantic, liberal writer: a position wholly and almost neatly opposed to that of Marilyn Butler and different again from that of Gilbert and Gubar.

Other feminist insights

Judith Lowder Newton, in a study called *Women, Power and Subversion: Social Strategies in British Fiction, 1778–1860* (1981, University of Georgia Press), looks at the way women's fiction deals with the problems of writing from within a patriarchal ideology. In writing about *Pride and Prejudice* she argues that although men are shown to have all the power and all the privilege, they nonetheless are shown to be both 'bungling and absurd'. In contrast the women, despite their lack of power, are not depicted as victims of their position. She also notes that 'the most authentically powerful figure in the novel is an unmarried, middle-class woman without a fortune' (reprinted in Clark, R., *ibid*, p. 124). There are very many essays and books which apply a feminist viewpoint to Austen's work. These include Rachel M. Brownstein, *Becoming a Heroine: Reading About Women in Novels* (1984, Penguin); Ellen Moers, *Literary Women* (1977, W. H. Allen) and Nina Auerbach, *Communities of Women: an Idea in Fiction* (1978, Harvard University Press).

NEW HISTORICISM

New Historicism takes its origins largely from the work of the French philosopher Michael Foucault and concerns itself with a reappraisal of the past and of what we mean by history. The traditional historical viewpoint tended to see the past as contained within a single story, a tale that could be told with endless certainty. New Historicism has argued against any notion of

> **KEYWORD**
>
> New Historicism: A theory which takes the view that there can be no historical certainty. The past can only be seen from within our own ideological present.

historic certainty. We cannot simply encapsulate the past within a single narrative; the past, like the present, is far more complex than this. The writings of Butler and Duckworth can certainly be seen as forerunners of this approach, although it did not really get going until the 1980s. Certainly John Wiltshire's *Jane Austen and the Body* (1972, Cambridge) is an example of this approach applied to Austen's novels. In it he looks at the way in which the novels engage with the body in all its many forms, particularly in relation to sickness and health but also as an expression of sexuality. Another would be Nancy Armstrong's *Desire and Domestic Fiction: A Political History of the Novel* (1987, Oxford University Press Inc. USA), particularly for the way it challenges Gilbert and Gubar and suggests that the 'domestic novel' may have been instrumental in offering women some sense of empowerment.

There certainly seems to be no fall in the critical and intellectual interest generated by Austen's six novels. New books offering new insights into the novels and the life of their author appear each year as do an astonishing number of academic articles in journals and on the Internet. What is certain is that post modernist readings of Austen offer not a single viewpoint, a certain and prescribed 'truth' but rather a diversity of opinions. Often these viewpoints will be at odds with each other, sometimes they will offer wholly new viewpoints and at other times they will simply retread familiar territory. In the final chapter of this book there are suggestions as to where to find some of these opinions and so continue to explore Austen's literary heritage.

✳ ✳ ✳ SUMMARY ✳ ✳ ✳

- Marilyn Butler and Alistair Duckworth both contributed to the politicalization of Austen's novels in the 1970s.

- Both writers saw her as being critically engaged in the political and social upheavals of her period.

- Post-structuralist accounts of Austen have offered new perspectives, particularly in exploring the gaps in her narrative.

- Feminist writers have identified Austen as a writer trapped in the patriarchal ideology of her period and also as a subversive, consciously reacting against this ideology.

- New Historicism stresses the multiplicity of history.

Where to next? 9

NOVELS

As there are only six completed novels it is comparatively easy to be well read in Austen! There are also the juvenilia as well as *Lady Susan*, the novel started in Bath but never finished and *Sanditon*, Austen's other unfinished novel, although there is a version which has been completed 'by another lady'. Certainly the part written by Austen is interesting as a first draft, but is nowhere up to the standard of the finished novels.

LETTERS

Jane Austen's letters published by Oxford paperbacks and edited by Deirdre Le Faye are a good read. Le Faye has added more material to the original Chapman editions and also rearranged the letters into their original chronological sequence. They are well annotated and provide a useful insight into the life and times of Austen and of her world. They also leave the question of just what might have been in the other letters destroyed by Cassandra!

BIOGRAPHIES

There are a number of very good biographies of Jane Austen. First there is the Austen-Leigh biography which is reprinted at the end of the Penguin Classic edition of *Persuasion*. Three more modern biographies are recommended: *Jane Austen: A Life*, Claire Tomalin (1997, Viking); *Jane Austen*, David Nokes (1997, Fourth Estate); or for readers wanting a shorter account of Austen's life written by a modern novelist there is *Jane Austen*, Carol Shields (2001, Weidenfeld & Nicolson). Of similar interest is Brian Southam's recent account of the influence of the Royal Navy on Jane Austen's life: *Jane Austen and the Navy* (2000, Hambledon and London).

CRITICAL WORKS

The two books of criticism which are still most widely cited are those by Marilyn Butler and Alistair Duckworth. The former is called *Jane Austen and the War of Ideas*, published by the Clarendon Press (OUP); the second is called *The Improvement of the Estate* and is published by the Johns Hopkins University Press.

There are some excellent collections of modern critical essays on the novels in the Casebook series. These are published by Macmillan: *Sense and Sensibility and Pride and Prejudice* edited by Robert Clark; *Emma* edited by David Monaghan; and *Mansfield Park and Persuasion* edited by Judy Simmons.

WEBSITES

By far the best website is The Republic of Pemberley **http://www.pemberley.com** – a great place for all those who enjoy discussing all aspects of Austen and her work. It has separate forums for each novel as well as forums to do with Austen's life and times. But BE WARNED they do not appreciate enquiries from students who want help with writing their essays.

The Jane Austen website **http://www.janeausten.co.uk/** hosted by the Jane Austen centre in Bath is also a good place to find information and links to other sites.

Electronic versions of all Austen's novels can be found at Project Gutenberg **http://promo.net/pg**

The Jane Austen museum website is
http://www.janeaustenmuseum.org.uk/

James Dawe's website has lots of information on films and books about Jane Austen as well as links to other sites.
http://www.jamesdawe.com/austen.html

PLACES TO VISIT

Jane Austen's cottage

The house where Austen lived in Chawton, near Alton, now houses the Jane Austen Museum and is more than worth a visit, particularly because it has not been commercialized but rather lovingly preserved by The Jane Austen Society. The address is Jane Austen's House, Chawton, Alton, Hampshire GU34 1SD, England. Telephone and Fax +44 (0) 1420 83262. It is open from March to December between 1.00 a.m. to 4.30 p.m. and from January to February at weekends and local school half-term days from 11.00 a.m. to 4.30 p.m.

Jane Austen Centre

This is a more commercialized exhibition but nonetheless well worth a visit. You can tour Bath and see the places where Jane Austen lived and wrote about. The visit also offers a permanent exhibition and a well-stocked gift shop full of Austen memorabilia. The address is 40 Gay Street, Bath BA1 2NT. Telephone +44 (0) 1225 443000.

JANE AUSTEN SOCIETY

The Jane Austen Society publishes a newsletter and also holds conferences, meetings and study days across the country about the life and work of Jane Austen. It is a good place to find out what is happening Austen-wise, particularly around the UK.

FILMS OF AUSTEN NOVELS

Pride and Prejudice has been filmed a number of times, the earliest being that directed by Robert Z. Leonard and starring Greer Garson as Elizabeth and Lawrence Olivier as Darcy. The 1999 TV adaptation written by Andrew Davies might be better suited to current tastes. Certainly Colin Firth's Darcy is about as sexy as Austen would have wished him. Look out, too, for David Bamber's sycophantic and bumptious Mr Collins. It is well filmed, well acted and a very good introduction to the novel.

Emma Thompson's version of *Sense and Sensibility* is another well-crafted adaptation. Thompson's Elinor is well matched by Kate Winslet's Marianne and Alan Rickman is masterful in the role of Colonel Brandon. In both these films the period is well captured. They also each manage to convey the pleasure of the Austen novel, although the elusive ironical wit is very hard to reproduce on the screen.

Emma has been less successfully adapted for film. The 1996 version with Gwyneth Paltrow is merely passable whilst the (again) Andrew Davies-scripted TV version of 1997 is considerably better. For a fun and different take on the story, you could try *Clueless*, a more successful Hollywood approach written and directed by Amy Heckerling in 1995 and described in the International Movie Database (IMDB) as 'Jane Austen's Emma meets Beverley Hills'.

The 1999 film version of *Mansfield Park* merges together certain aspects of Austen's own life with that of Fanny Price. It uses both stories to create a new one and does so with considerable success. It makes quite a few changes along the way. The semi-naked lesbian love scene between Mary Crawford and Fanny Price, for example, is something of a striking departure from the original!

A far more unusual adaptation of an Austen novel can be found in the film *Kandukondein Kandukondein,* an adaptation of *Sense and Sensibility* by Indian filmmaker Rajiv Menon. It is set in contemporary Indian society and is much more than merely a film about love. It is, as you might imagine, very different from the Austen novel but beautifully filmed and with exceptional performances by Tabu and Aishwarya Rai who play the two sisters.

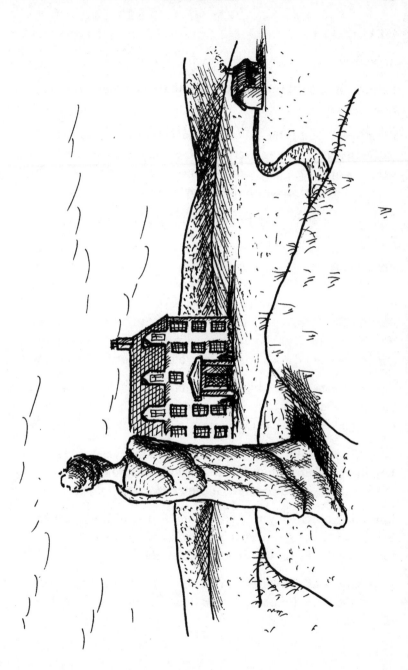

GLOSSARY

Aphorism A pithy expression, saying or maxim.

Bathos A descent from the elevated to the commonplace for comic effect.

Burlesque This is the ridiculing of an existing form of writing, traditionally by treating a serious subject in a light-hearted way. In writing a burlesque of this form Austen is mocking the far-fetched plots and clichéd scenarios that many of these novels adopted.

Canon The body of writing that is accepted as representative of a period or culture.

Entailment Entailing restricted what a son could do with an estate when he inherited. It forced him to leave the land to his eldest son. An entailed estate could not be sold nor mortgaged and so could only be used for the purposes of maintaining an income by being farmed or rented. An estate could only be entailed across two generations so a grandfather could entail his estate to his grandson but not beyond.

Enlightenment The philosophical movement that took place in Europe (particularly in France) in the eighteenth century in which reason and individualism were emphasized at the expense of tradition.

Epiphany A word coined by James Joyce used to describe a moment in which an experience reveals its inner meaning.

Epistolary novel A novel written in the form of letters. Aphra Behn's *Love Letters between a Nobleman and his Sister* and Richardson's *Pamela* are two examples of the form.

An **eponymous** hero or heroine is one whose name appears in the title of the work, for example, Don Juan, Robinson Crusoe, The Mayor of Casterbridge.

Fallible or unreliable narrator   This is often used in novels written in the first person to mislead the reader by presenting something about which the narrator is mistaken as a seeming truth. *The Catcher in the Rye* and *The Great Gatsby* are obvious modern examples. Austen narrates her novels in the third person but her (again early) use of free indirect discourse means that the viewpoint of the narrator and that of the heroine are often difficult to separate.

Feminism   The study of gender politics from a female perspective. Usually the term is applied to the political and social movement which swept Western Europe and the United States beginning in the late 1960s.

Free indirect discourse   A narrative style in which the narrator presents the thoughts of a character. In direct speech we should read, 'Emma said, "I am feeling unwell"'. In indirect speech the sentence would be rendered, 'Emma said she felt unwell.' In free indirect speech it would be simply, 'Emma felt unwell.'

Gothic novel   A form that became very popular in the second half of the eighteenth century. The stories usually involve a frail, beautiful heroine who finds herself in some peril in a haunted castle, abbey, graveyard and who invites rescue, preferably from the dashing young hero.

Gynocriticism   This focuses on women writers in an attempt to challenge traditionally male-defined (and male-dominated) literary canon. It looks at what defines and distinguishes female writing from its male counterpart.

Ideology   A system of ideas or representations that dominate the conscious, and often unconscious, minds of groups and individuals.

Irony   A statement in which the apparent meaning is undermined by one or more other meanings which arise from understanding the statement from within the context in which it is placed.

Jacobin   A term derived from the French Revolution. The Jacobins were a French political society established in 1789 at the old Dominican convent in Paris. The term is usually synonymous with 'revolutionary'.

Magical realism   Fiction which disrupts the apparent reality of events in a novel with the impossible and the miraculous. The novels of Salman Rushdie and Gabriel Garcia Marquez are seen as examples of this genre.

New Historicism   A theory which takes the view that there can be no historical certainty. The past can only be seen from within our own ideological present.

Novel   The modern novel developed quite slowly through the memoir novel and the epistolic novel (written in the form of letters) during the sixteenth and seventeenth century. The eighteenth century saw this develop into the novel written often in the third person in the works of writers such as Defoe, Felding, Smollett and Richardson.

Post-structuralist   The term is often used synonymously with Deconstuctionism, a movement led by Jacques Derrida, Roland Barthes, the post-Freudian analysts Jacques Lacan and Julia Kristeva and the historical crtiques of Michael Foucault amongst others. It argues for what is called the instability of meanings where there are no fixed points, no absolutes and no hierarchies but rather a lot of uncertainty and what is called plurality or free play. It rejects the idea of there being an intrinsic meaning within a text which can be extracted by means of careful analysis.

Primogeniture   The right of primogeniture meant that all the land in a family was left to only the eldest son.

Protagonist   The chief character in a play or story.

Satire   To use satire is to ridicule often by exaggerating the traits of a character to expose them as failings or weaknesses. It is usually used for humorous effect but can often have a more serious purpose.

A **signifier** or a **sign** is a label which suggests a **signified** or an object in the real world. For example, the sign created by the three letters 'c – o – w' suggests a four-legged beast which chews grass and produces milk.

Structuralism A movement which emphasized the functions of language and the patterns found within it. Language is seen as a self-contained system of signs in which meaning is found in the fact that one sign is different from another. So the word 'door' is different from the word 'window', but both are seen as arbitrary labels for things in the world.

Symbolism The use of image or concept to represent another.

Mary Wollstonecraft (1759–97) Early radical fighter for women's rights and mother of Mary Shelley. Her most famous work was *A Vindication of the Rights of Women* published in 1792 and which attacked the way in which women's education kept them passive and ignorant. It was most likely read by Austen and probably influenced *Mansfield Park*.

Chronology of major works

Possibly 1796	Finishes *Lady Susan*
	Begins *First Impressions* in October
1795	Begins work on *Elinor and Marianne*
1797	*First Impressions* refused by Cadell, a London publisher
	Elinor and Marianne revised for first time
1798–9	*Northanger Abbey* written
1803	*Northanger Abbey* sold to Richard Crosby for £10 with the title *Susan* but not published
	Begins work on her unfinished novel, *The Watsons*
1809	'Elinor and Marianne' revised for second time
1811	*Sense and Sensibility* published
	Begins work on *Mansfield Park*
1813	*Pride and Prejudice* published
1814	Austen begins writing *Emma*
	Mansfield Park published
1815–16	*Persuasion* written
1816	Henry Austen buys back *Susan*
	Emma published
1817	*Susan* revised as *Northanger Abbey*
	Northanger Abbey and *Persuasion* published as a set of four volumes

FURTHER READING

Armstrong, Nancy *Desire and Domestic Fiction: A Political History of the Novel* (Oxford University Press Inc. USA, 1987)

Auerbach, Nina *Communities of Women: an Idea in Fiction* (Harvard University Press, 1978)

Browstein, Rachel M *Becoming a Heroine: Reading About Women in Novels* (Penguin, 1984)

Butler, M *Jane Austen and the War of Ideas* (OUP, 1975)

Clark, R (ed.) *New Casebook: Sense and Sensibility and Pride and Prejudice* (Macmillan, 1994)

Copeland, C and MacMaster, J (ed.) *The Cambridge Companion to Jane Austen* (CUP, 1997)

Duckworth, A *The Improvement of the Estate* (Johns Hopkins University Press, 1994)

Gilbert, S and Gubar, S *The Madwoman in the Attic: The Woman Writer and Nineteenth Century Literary Imagination* (New Haven, 1979)

Kirkham, Margaret *Jane Austen, Feminism and Fiction* (Athlone Press, 1997)

Moers, Ellen *Literary Women* (W H Allen, 1977)

Monaghan, D (ed.) *New Casebook: Emma* (Macmillan, 1992)

Nokes, David *Jane Austen* (Fourth Estate, 1997)

Shields, Carol *Jane Austen* (Weidenfield & Nicolson, 2001)

Simmons, J, *New Casebook: Mansfield Park and Persuasion* (Macmillan, 1997)

Southam, B, *Jane Austen: The Critical Heritage, Volumes 1 & 2 1870 –1940* (Routledge and Kegan Paul, 1987)

Southam, Brian *Jane Austen and the Navy* (Hambledon and London, 2000)

Tomalin, Claire *Jane Austen: A Life* (Viking, 1997)

Wiltshire, John *Jane Austen and the Body* (Cambridge, 1972)

INDEX

D. H. LAWRENCE – A BEGINNER'S GUIDE

Jenny Weatherburn

D. H. Lawrence – A Beginner's Guide introduces you to the life and works of this eminent and prolilfic writer. Lawrence's ideas and themes are clearly outlined with reference to his major novels, short stories and poems; useful quotations from Lawrence's essays and letters are brought in to help give you a more complete picture of this man and his work.

Jenny Weatherburn's informative text explores:

- how to approach the novels, short stories and poems
- the way in which Lawrence's writing was influenced by his own life
- his ideas about nature and industrialization
- contemporary critical approaches to Lawrence and his work
- the influence of Lawrence both in his own lifetime and in the twenty-first century

T. S. ELIOT –
A BEGINNER'S GUIDE

Alistair Wisker

Eliot – A Beginner's Guide introduces you to the life and works of this eminent and prolific writer. By exploring some of his major works the writer shows the relevance of Eliot today and helps you to develop your own responses to the works.

Alistair Wisker's lively text explores:

- how to approach the novels, short stories and poems

- ideas about the activity of writing and the activity of reading and the connections between the two

- contemporary critical approaches to Eliot and his work

- the influence of Eliot both in his own lifetime and in the twenty-first century.